Getting Beginners to Talk

JIM WINGATE

Prentice Hall
New York   London   Toronto   Sydney   Tokyo   Singapore

PRENTICE HALL INTERNATIONAL ENGLISH LANGUAGE TEACHING

First published 1993 by
Prentice Hall Europe
Campus 400, Maylands Avenue
Hemel Hempstead
Hertfordshire, HP2 7EZ
A division of
Simon & Schuster International Group

© International Book Distributors Ltd.

Typeset in 10½/12½pt Times
by MHL Typesetting Ltd, Coventry

Printed in Great Britain by Redwood Books,
Trowbridge, Wiltshire

Library of Congress Cataloging-in-Publication Data

Wingate, Jim.
    Getting beginners to talk / Jim Wingate.
       p.   cm. — (Language teaching methodology series)
  (English language teaching)
    Includes index.
    ISBN 0-13-357708-2 : $12.96
    1. English language—Study and teaching—Foreign speakers.
  2. English language—Spoken English. I. Title. II. Series.
  III. Series: English language teaching (Englewood Cliffs, N.J.).
  PE1128.A2W56   1993   92-29720
                                     CIP

British Library Cataloguing in Publication Data

A catalogue record for this book is available from the British Library

ISBN 0-13-357708-2 (pbk)

---

6 7 8 9   01 00 99 98

Contents

PART TWO: ACTIVITIES, ROLE-PLAYS, SIMULATIONS AND DISCUSSIONS

Indexes

Thanks and acknowledgements

My warm thanks go to Pilgrims Language Courses, Canterbury and the many fellow teachers I have learned from through team teaching and demonstration lessons over the last 15 years: Mark Thistlewood, Paul Fagg, Judy Baker, Kevin Batchelor, Rick Cooper, Michael Gradwell, Tessa Woodward, Janet Ohana, Mario Rinvolucri, John Morgan, Jean-Paul Creton, James Dixey, Cynthia Beresford, David Hill, Mick Reid, Imelda Harling, Sue Greetham, Rene Bosewitz, Gerry Kenny, Penny Ur and Andrew Wright.

I am particularly grateful to the British Council Chester and Leeds and the BBC summer schools where I have been able to pilot techniques, and to the beginner Pilgrims students from Spain and Japan and students in Germany, Sweden, Austria, Greece and Israel who have helped to teach me what works and what doesn't work.

I am very lucky to work with thousands of teachers in 10 different countries every year. I have absorbed their good ideas like a sponge. I'm sorry if I can't remember where each good idea originally came from, but I thank you all for sharing so freely. That's what networks are for. Through this book I am now sharing back to you.

Introduction

Many teachers want to teach English communicatively but feel that their students must know at least a few hundred words before communicative methods can be used. In *Getting Beginners to Talk*, by contrast, we work communicatively from the start with total beginners.

Getting Beginners to Talk is the companion volume to *Getting Students to Talk* by Aleksandra Gołębiowska. *Getting Beginners to Talk* is designed to help teachers of students from beginners to upper elementary whereas *Getting Students to Talk* is designed to help teachers of students from upper elementary to upper intermediate and advanced.

Getting Beginners to Talk is divided into two parts. Part One is itself divided into two sections:

- First Principles — which introduces techniques, principles, worked examples and tips for teaching beginners communicatively

- Practicalities — which outlines practical ways of using this book alongside your course book.

Part Two is a collection of specific techniques and lesson plans for teaching beginners and encouraging them to speak English. It is based on a series of activities followed by linking role-plays, simulations and discussions.

At the end of the book, indexes list the activities under *grammar, vocabulary* and *function* so that you can dip into the book to supplement the particular item you are teaching.

I hope you and your students find all the lesson ideas in Part Two interesting. You are welcome to write to me c/o the publisher with your comments, reactions and any other ideas.

The aims of this book

If you want to 'get your beginners to talk' this book is for you. It suggests practical ways in which you can help your students learn more quickly, practical ways in which *you can teach* more effectively, practical ways of using the *classroom* chairs and tables, and practical ways of using your *course book*. It also contains many practical lessons and lesson ideas.

Aim 1   The students

The aim of this book is to help your students to be confident, communicative and interested. It will help your students to listen to what you say the first time you say it, and remember to use what you say. It will also help your students to use their own intelligence fully, and to become more responsible for their own learning and for correcting themselves.

Aim 2   The classroom

The aim is to have a classroom where the students speak much more than the teacher, and where the students talk to one another, really communicating what they want to say, and doing it in English. The activities in the classroom will have purpose and control arising from the students' own self-discipline and co-operation. There will be time too for silence, for thought, and for quiet listening.

Aim 3   The teacher

This book aims to take the pressure off you. At the moment you may be working too hard and your students may not be working hard enough. By getting your beginners to talk, using the techniques in this book, you are set free to teach and to make rapid progress with your students. It is no longer you who has to do most of the talking, motivating, organising and thinking. Your students will gradually learn to do much more of this for themselves.

Aim 4   The course book

Even the best course books have not been written about the particular students in your classroom. Your students are much more motivated to practise the present perfect simple if they are given an opportunity to talk about themselves rather than about Mr and Mrs Brown in the course book who go shopping. This book helps you to adapt the course book to make it relevant to your students.

Aim 5   The lessons

To fulfil these aims we have to turn one tradition upside down. This is that the words have to be taught before they are used in communication. In this book the communication comes first, often without words. Then the words are added. This means that the lessons are firstly about conveying meaning and only then about using new words.

PART ONE

USING THE MATERIAL

Using the material

This book is intended to be used alongside your course book. The diagram below gives you a visual guide as to how you might be able to combine the two. Ask yourself the questions shown in the diagram about each course book lesson as you are preparing it.

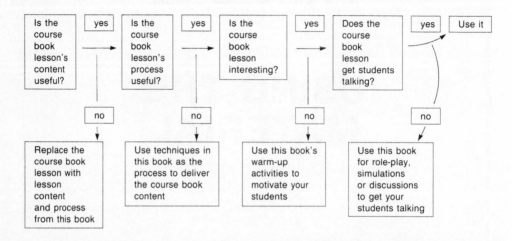

The techniques in this book are processes which you can use to deliver any appropriate content from the course book. They include Concentric Circles, Action Chains, mimes, noises, story-telling, gestures and intonation and can be used to teach any new item. As you use more of the specific techniques in this book they will become part of your general repertoire and extend your potential as a teacher. However, don't try to adapt a specific technique until you have used it as it is demonstrated in this book. To use a technique from this book as the process to deliver course book content requires no mental effort at all once you have already used that technique with its own content.

Finding your way in this book

Part One is divided into two sections:

- First Principles — designed to get you started. This section outlines a series of principles for teaching beginners. Each principle is demonstrated in one or more worked examples displayed like this:

Worked example 1

- Practicalities — designed to show you how to use the activities in Part Two of this book. This section explains some of the reasoning behind the approach that has been adopted.

Part One also includes many diagrams designed to present a visual explanation of the principle being outlined and helpful tips on using the material. These are displayed as follows:

Diagram 1.

TIP:

Principles for teaching beginners are often highlighted in *italics*.

Part Two is a rich resource of classroom material. It includes activities, role-plays, simulations and discussions with full instructions for you the teacher.

There is also a *contents* list at the beginning of this book and *indexes* at the end, listing all the activities under *grammar, vocabulary* and *function* so that you can scan one or more index and find an appropriate lesson idea.

First principles

How to start a lesson

You could write on the board at the beginning of a lesson 'The present simple tense of the verb to be'. Or you could write 'Jobs and work'. It's the same lesson, but 'Jobs and work' is easier for your students to relate to than the grammar label. You could then write 'pop star, boss, rock singer, movie star, computer programmer' because these are specific recognisable names of jobs they know already without having to learn them. In this way you will have got your students thinking on the topic of jobs. By doing this you will teach them the present simple and they'll use it. At the end of the lesson tell them the name of the tense if you like. Some students like classifying new things.

> TIP: Try to give your students a topic or theme they can relate to immediately as a way of introducing each lesson. If they can relate to it, they will want to talk about it. They will also *want* to use the new vocabulary and grammar which you teach.

You have also guaranteed that your lesson will be a success rather than set yourself up for failure. If you say 'This lesson is about the present simple tense' and by the end of the lesson your students are *not* using the present simple, then *they* know and *you* know that the lesson has failed. If, instead, you say 'This lesson is about jobs and work' and at the end of the lesson they are not using the present simple, it has still been an interesting and useful lesson talking about jobs and work, and you can say to yourself 'Mm, I'll try teaching the present simple a different way tomorrow'. The lesson *was* a success because it *was* about jobs and work.

Here are two worked example lesson starters to do when your students already have ten words for clothes.

Worked example 1

Starting a topic-based lesson

Lesson aim: To teach 'borrow' and 'lend'
Time: 5–10 minutes
Preparation: A hat or scarf you can lend. Invitations to a fancy dress party

1. Write on the board 'A party' (not 'borrow' and 'lend').

2. Give out invitations and say 'Here's your invitation, here's yours, here's your invitation etc. Let me read it. Yes, an invitation to a party. "Fancy dress". Ah, costume, special clothes: "Dress as someone from History". Great! Who shall I be? Alexander the Great? Cleopatra? John the Baptist? Napoleon? Ah, but what shall I wear? Clothes, special clothes. Has anybody got a big coat they can lend me? Maria, can you lend me a big coat? No? Bruno, please lend me a big coat so I can be Napoleon. I'll give it back to you after the party'.

3. Ask each student who they would like to be. Keep offering to lend your hat and scarf.

4. So far your students have been silently listening to you using and demonstrating 'lend' and 'borrow'. Now they talk, deciding what they will wear, and then they go round asking to borrow the items they need.

Worked example 2

Starting a topic-based lesson

Lesson aim: To teach 'borrow' and 'lend'
Time: 5–10 minutes
Preparation: An item of clothing, e.g. skirt, and slips of paper as money

1. Write on the board 'shopping' (not 'borrow' and 'lend').

2.   Say 'Tell me words'. The students then brainstorm words to do with shopping. You write the words on the board.

3.   Say 'It's my sister's birthday tomorrow. Oh dear, what shall I buy? I've only got five pounds. That (skirt) looks nice. My sister will like that. Oh dear, it's six pounds. Six pounds! Er, can anybody lend me one pound? Maria, can you lend me one pound? I'll pay you back tomorrow. No? Bruno, can you lend me one pound? The skirt is six pounds. I've only got five pounds. Can you lend me one pound? I'll pay you back tomorrow'.

4.   Then each student takes off something — a watch, bracelet, shoe, sweater. You put a price slip on each thing, e.g. £10, but you only give each student a slip of paper representing £5 so that in order to buy they have to borrow the difference.

TIP: Don't be afraid to say sentences using some words your students don't already know. That's no problem for them if the message of the sentence is clear.

Focus your lesson on a topic or theme your students can relate to.

Experience not explanation

Remember we're starting with the message then adding the words and the grammar. In the worked examples on 'borrow' and 'lend' I don't expect my students to understand every word I say. What I want is for them to experience the situation and to understand the idea of borrow and lend through that experience. So I don't say to them 'Today's lesson is on borrow and lend. I'll explain. When you borrow you are the needy recipient in a bilateral and temporary change of user situation for the borrowed item but where the proprietoriality has not changed. Whereas when you lend . . .' Obviously, that is an exaggeration but even in their mother tongue an explanation like that would be difficult for the students, and not helpful to their understanding.
   Start with the message then add the words and the grammar.

'Sowing seeds'

TIP: Instead of explaining, try giving your students an experience of the new vocabulary or grammar *in the previous lesson*. Don't teach it, just use it in a natural way.

Worked example 3

Sowing seeds for learning 'borrow' and 'lend' in the next lesson

Lesson aim: Experience of 'borrow' and 'lend'
Time: 3 minutes
Preparation: Lose your pen

1. Say 'Oh dear, I've lost my pen (gestures and looking for it). I want to write. Can I borrow somebody's pen? Maria, can I borrow your pen? Thanks'. Write 'Thank you for lending me your pen'. Give the pen back.

2. Later in the lesson borrow another pen from another student to write something else, and say similar sentences.

Worked example 4

Sowing seeds for learning 'borrow' and 'lend' in the next lesson

Lesson aim: Experience of 'borrow' and 'lend'
Time: 3 minutes
Preparation: In the previous lesson ask students to bring coloured pens/pencils to this lesson. You bring coloured pens/pencils too.

1. In any exercise using different coloured pens or pencils, some students will not have all the colours they need. You can go round lending your pens or pencils and encouraging them to lend theirs to each other. Say 'Ah Bruno you need a green and a red. I'll lend you my green. Here it is. I'll want it back at the end of the lesson. Can you borrow a red from Maria?'

By sowing seeds in this way your students will hear and understand the new vocabulary or grammar that you will teach in the next lesson. Unconsciously they feel at ease with it, and they learn it much faster.

Say the new words and grammar in a natural situation in the lesson before the lesson you teach them in.

True examples

Bruno has borrowed my green pen. If I then tell him to 'lend' it to Maria, that's not really lending. The green pen is not Bruno's to lend. Therefore my example is not true.

If I walk round the classroom and ask 'What am I doing?', my students answer 'Walking' or 'You are walking', but if when *I ask* the question I stop walking, 'You are walking' is not true. 'You are standing still' or 'You have just stopped walking' *are* true.

> TIP: It is important that the examples you teach are true when you teach them. Then the grammar or vocabulary concepts will be understood correctly by your students.

Teach examples which are correct and true.

Learner diaries

Taking truth one step further, ask your students to write a sentence for each new word and each new grammar item. Each student writes the sentence in their 'grammar diary' or 'learner diary'. There are two rules for entries in their diaries:

- Each sentence must be about themselves, i.e. autobiographical
- Each sentence must be true.

This 'personalises' each new word or grammar item, and integrates the new language into your students' own experiences.

It also gives your students automatic homework. For example, you could ask them to read through their learner diary and prepare to talk about themselves for five minutes using their learner diary. Or they could borrow someone else's learner diary, read it and talk about that person at the next lesson. These two homeworks provide practice of the first person singular and the third person singular. If pairs borrow each other's diaries and then talk to each other they will be practising the second person singular and first person plural. If they then report to others they will be using the third person plural.

Students write examples which are true and about themselves.

Concentric Circles

Concentric Circles is one of the physical classroom techniques for getting your beginners to talk. In Concentric Circles the students keep meeting different people and are therefore happy to say the same thing several times. Diagrams 1, 2 and 3 show how Concentric Circles work.

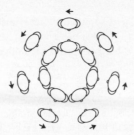

Explanation
Each student  is facing a partner. First, the students say their sentences. Then all the outside circle students move round one place to their right and say their sentences again. Then they move another place to their right and say their sentences again.

Diagram 1.   Standing, 14 students

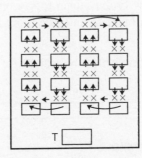

Explanation
☐ = chair → = student moving. Three repetitions of the same task is enough. Each time it is to a different person. If there is an odd number, you join in.

Diagram 2.   Concentric Circles, 28 students sitting in loose chairs

☐ = desk   x = student   T = teacher
→ = that student moving to a new partner

Explanation
To signal the outside students to move round, clap your hands. All the outside students move at the same time.

Diagram 3.   Concentric Circles, 32 students in fixed chairs at desks

TIP: You can keep trouble-makers apart so that they never meet! Get each student to write their name on a piece of paper. Put one name in each place making sure the trouble-makers are in the *same* circle but *not next* to each other.

TIP: You can use Concentric Circles for mixed level work. For example, put all the 'higher' students in the inside circle and all the 'lower' students in the outside circle. Then they are always paired lower with higher to help each other, and speak English together.

The following worked examples show how you can use Concentric Circles in your lessons.

Worked example 5

Concentric Circles for dialogue practice

Lesson aim: Speaking practice
Time: 5 minutes

1. In the very first lessons, make Concentric Circles towards the end of each lesson.

2. Say (in English with gestures to your watch, or in your students' mother tongue) 'You are going to speak English for three minutes'. Prompt them to say specific sentences they have learned as dialogue, e.g. introductions. Immediately move outside students round one place and ask them to repeat the sentences. Move them again and repeat. Move them again but this time prompt them to say other specific sentences as dialogue. Again move them twice more and repeat, and so on.

3. Say 'Stop! You have been speaking English (show watch) for four minutes! Well done!'

Worked example 6

Concentric Circles for question and answer practice

Lesson aim: Question and answer practice
Time: 5 minutes

1.   Make Concentric Circles.

2.   Tell the outside students to ask and the inside students to answer. Give them the question to ask. The outside students ask it and the inside students answer. Move the outside students round. Tell the inside students to ask the same question. Move the outside students round. Tell them to ask and answer the question again. Change the question. Move the outside students round and tell them to ask the new question, and so on. (When the form of the question is known, you need only say the topic/subject of the question. Your students can substitute the new topic in the old question, e.g. 'Have you got a bicycle? . . . sister? . . . brother? . . . car?'

To increase speaking practice change pairs frequently.

Action Chains

We saw in Concentric Circles a technique you can use in any or every lesson to *practise* what has been learned. By using Action Chains, you can *teach* new vocabulary.

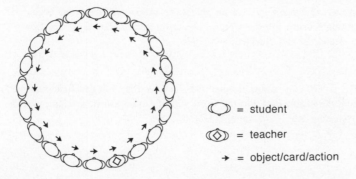

◯ = student

◉ = teacher

→ = object/card/action

Explanation
1. Pass a picture to the first student with a *gesture* (e.g. if flowers, you smell them). That student passes it to the next student with the same gesture, and so on until you receive it back with the gesture from the last student.
2. Send the picture round as before with the gesture but this time add the *target word*, e.g. 'smell'.
3. Send the picture round with the gesture and the target word *in a sentence*, e.g. 'I am smelling the flowers.'
4. If in step 2 or 3 the last student gives you the wrong word or sentence, send it round again correctly.
5. As soon as one picture is going round in step 1 you can send another one round with its gesture so that there is a flow of between four and eight pictures with gesture, gesture and word and word in a sentence.

Diagram 4.   Action Chains, Action Chain in a standing or sitting circle

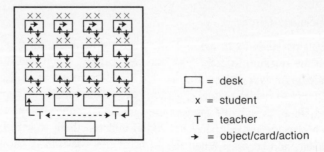

= desk

x = student

T = teacher

→ = object/card/action

Diagram 5.   Action Chain, 32 students in fixed chairs at desks

In an Action Chain your students first experience and understand the message, then you add the word, then they hear and say the word in a sentence. (It doesn't matter if they don't understand all the other words in the sentence.) When they are confident of all the sentences, begin to pass some pictures and sentences in one direction while you pass the others the other way at the same time. This is an extra challenge especially for the student who is given two cards and sentences to pass on from two directions at once! With the Action Chain technique you are only teaching one student at a time. That student then teaches the next and so on.

TIP: You can pass round a *picture* or an *object*, or an *action*. Nearly all beginners' words can be taught using either a picture, object, or action. Examples are flowers and smell, food and eat and saucepan and cook.

TIP: If there is a 'difficult' sound in one of the new words, you can first send just the sound along the chain, *then* add the word with the sound in it. Example sounds are 'th', 's', 'sh' and 'ch'.

Worked example 7

Action Chain

Lesson aim: Vocabulary
Time: 5−10 minutes
Preparation: Between four and eight picture cards

1. Produce picture cards showing different objects, e.g. flowers, food, saucepan.

2. Make a circle or equivalent and pass picture A to the first student with a gesture, e.g. flowers and smell.

3. The student passes it on to the next student with the same gesture.

4. Pass picture B to the first student with a gesture and so on until all the pictures are going round.

5. When picture A comes to the last student, pass it to the first student again with the word and gesture. The first student then passes it on saying the word and doing the gesture. Do the same with the other pictures.

6. When picture A comes to the last student again, pass it to the first student again with the word in a sentence. Do the same with the other pictures.

7. When the last picture comes to the last student again start passing the pictures and sentences around the class in both directions.

Give your students time to experience and handle the thing before you teach the word for it.

Pronunciation

Using Action Chains you can pass a 'difficult' sound along the chain before you pass the word with the difficult sound in it. The students have to listen very carefully because you say each word only once. If they say the word correctly, you don't need to say it more than once. Obviously if they get it wrong, you send the word along again correctly pronounced. To help them get the pronunciation right, send the *corrected* pronunciation of a word both ways along a chain at once.

You might also enjoy chanting 'difficult' sounds with your students before they meet them in words. Mix difficult sounds with easy ones. Practise having your students chanting loud and soft and let them mix sounds and notes.

TIP: Ask each student to cup their two hands so that their words go from their mouth to their ear. When you say a new word in class, tell them to say it three times to themselves using cupped hands. In this way they hear themselves not others.

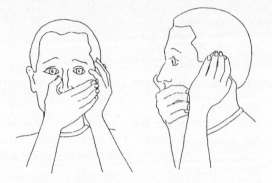

Diagram 6. Cupped hands

New sounds can be practised before the words which contain them.

Mime first, words later

In this exercise you don't speak at all until you have communicated. Your students don't speak either until they have already heard the words and have communicated several times without words.

Worked example 8

Mime first, words later

Lesson aim: Teaching vocabulary, e.g. I like ... I don't like ...
Time: 5–10 minutes

1. Point to yourself. (I) Put your hands on your heart (like). Mime reading a book (reading).

2. Point to yourself. (I) Frown, raise your top lip (don't like). Mime smoking a cigarette (smoking).

3. Mime in this way two more things you like and two more you don't like.

4. The students then mime in pairs their likes and dislikes to each other. While they are miming you go round miming to pairs more of your own likes and dislikes.

5. The students change pairs and mime again and then change pairs and mime again. During this second and third miming, you go round saying the words they are communicating in their mime. For

example, 'Ah Maria, you like swimming, you don't like dancing', or 'Bruno, you like smoking, you don't like swimming'.

6. Make a circle. Do your mimes again and say the sentences this time. Each student in turn then does one mime and you say each mime as a sentence. In the circle each in turn does another mime and you say the sentences.

7. The students make new pairs and say sentences as they mime. They then make new pairs and repeat.

8. Make the circle again. This time each person in turn does and says their own mime. Then everybody else repeats that person's sentence (remembering it).

9. The students make groups of three and say their likes and dislikes without the mimes.

Notice that the first time your students speak in the worked example above they are speaking very privately. They are not exposed. They are not being tested, they are communicating real messages about themselves.

TIP: If you want to practise second and third person singular and first and second and third person plural, the students can simply tell each other about other students' likes and dislikes.

There are many words you can teach through mime. Here are some examples:

Nouns	Pronouns	Verbs	More verbs	Adjectives	Adverbs	Prepositions
food	I	eat	like	big	slowly	in
drink	you	drink	don't like	small	quickly/fast	on
knife	he	drive	walk	light	quietly	below
pen/pencil	she	put ón	run	heavy	loudly	above
football	it	take off	stand	cold	well	off
tennis	we	swim	sit	hot	badly	out
swimming	you	wash	buy	tall	clumsily	into
bicycle	they	sleep	sell	short	carefully	onto
motorcycle	him	yawn	point at/to	quiet	sleepily	through
television	her	sniff	pick up	loud	eagerly	around
cassette tape	them	sneeze	drop	open	sadly	up
music	me	cough	ride	closed	happily	down

Think how you could mime each of these words. Can you see how you can mime sentences by putting words together? How could you put five or six sentences together to teach in one lesson under a particular topic or theme?

People can communicate without words.

Story-telling with mime

Think how you could tell a story in mime, then tell it again with just the target words, then tell it again with the target words in sentences, then tell it again with just the sentences and without the mime. A worked example follows.

Worked example 9

Story-telling with mime

Lesson aim: Present simple for everyday actions
Time: 10−15 minutes

1. Mime without words. Every day I *get up*. I get out of *bed*. I *wash*. I clean my *teeth*. I brush my *hair*. I go into the kitchen and make a cup of *coffee* and some *toast*. I put on my *clothes* and leave the *house*.

2. Mime again and say the words in italics as you mime.

3. Mime again but say the whole sentences as above.

4. Say the whole story without mime.

5. Mime without words. Invite your students to say the words while you mime.

6. Mime without words and invite your students to say the sentences.

7. Put your students in pairs to mime the same story to each other in turn and to say sentences for their mimes.

8. In their pairs they repeat this but instead they mime their own getting up routine. You go round giving them new words if they need them, e.g. 'yawn'.

TIP: You could do this in an Action Chain.

To mime is to survive in a strange country.

Message first, words later

Instead of silent gestures or mimes you can use English noises. Here are some English noises with their conventional spellings and gestures.

Noise	Meaning	Accompanying gesture
tut tut	disapproval, scolding	wagging index finger
huh!	put down, mockery	toss of head
ow!	sharp pain caused by another person	frown, look at person
ouch!	sharp pain not caused by another	frown, look at location of pain
uh huh!	mild agreement	slight nod of head
mmm!	approval, pleasure	smile
mmm!	doubtful agreement	downturned mouth, eyebrows raised
ugh!	disgust, revulsion	curled up upper lip
yuck!	disgust	open mouth, turn away
bah!	anger, dismissal	eyebrows up, toss of head
uh uh!	don't do it	shake of head
uh uh!	oh dear, trouble	eyebrows raised
argh!	(scream) fear, shock, surprise	wide open mouth and eyes
oof!	receiving a blow to body	frown, bend body to the blow
eh!	question, disbelief	open mouth

When you combine a noise with the gesture and a clear stimulus, the meaning is clear and communicates well. If your students use these noises they are communicating in very informal, real English. When they can communicate using the noises, then you can teach them *words, phrases* and *sentences* which express the same meaning in more formal English.

Look at the noises above and think of some words or sentences you could add, e.g. 'Yuck! Disgusting! This food is disgusting! I can't eat it!'

Worked example 10

Message first, words later

Lesson aim: To teach the function of complimenting. To practise vocabulary of clothing
Time: 3−5 minutes

1. The students should be standing all together.

2. Touch a garment or jewellery that you like on a student, smile and say 'Mmm'. Repeat with another student.

3. Encourage your students to circulate and ask them do the same to one another for 20 seconds.

4. Now do what you did before but instead say 'That's nice!' and encourage your students to do the same for 30 seconds and to respond by saying 'Thank you'.

5. Now do what you did before and say 'I like your ...', naming the garment or jewellery etc. Encourage your students to circulate and do the same for 45 seconds and to respond by saying 'Thank you'.

6. Repeat step 5 and continue the dialogue as follows:
    You: I like your ...
    Student: Thank you.
    You: Where did you get it?
    Student: ...
    Encourage your students to circulate and do the same for 90 seconds.

You can, if you prefer split this activity up over a number of lessons.

TIP: Giving a compliment is a good way of getting reserved English people into a conversation so teach it also as a 'conversation opener'.

Your students have an opportunity to say a new word for the first time to each other, not exposed to the whole class. Noises with gestures is survival in a strange country.

Intonation is meaning

People can be very expressive with very few words. Even in the very first lesson with your beginners you can encourage them to be expressive with intonation. They usually already know words like 'OK', 'yes', 'no' and 'love' *before* their first lesson of English.

Worked example 11

Intonation is meaning

Lesson aim: Expressiveness with intonation. Fun dialogues in the very first lesson

Time: 5–8 minutes

1. Do 30 seconds of chorussing 'OK', 'yes' and 'no'.

2. The students then use cupped hands (see Diagram 6) and repeat your word and intonation three times to themselves. You say:

   OK↘; OK?↗; OK−; OK∿; Yes↘; Yes?↗; Yes−; Yes∿; No↘; No No No No No ----; No?↗; No∿

3. Ask a confident student to come forward and model a dialogue where you both argue using only 'yes', 'no' and 'OK'.

4. Get the students to do the same in pairs (in their own ways).

In subsequent lessons you can add more English words, phrases and sentences which mean the same as the intonation, e.g. OK ; All right ; If you like ; I said I would ; e.g. OK? ; Is that all right? ; Are you sure? .

TIP: Older beginners can say 'yes', 'no', 'OK', and 'love' in lots of different ways!

Here are two poems. Try saying them aloud a few times trying different intonations.

Poem

Yes means yes
No means no
OK means yes and no

No means yes
Yes means no
OK means yes and no

OK means yes
OK means no
OK means OK OK

Yes? No? OK?
OK

Poem

Love, yes
Love, no
Love, OK

No. Yes Love.

No love. Yes?

Yes love. No.

OK love OK.

Love
Love

Read one of the poems in the first lesson with beginners. Get them to say it your way, then in their own ways in pairs. Get them to make up their own poems, and to say them in pairs.

Intonation is survival in a strange country.

Summary so far

Do you see how with gesture, mime, noises and intonation you have helped your students to achieve real communication? You have truly equipped them to survive. They *can* communicate. So far too, they know they can *understand* what you say even if they don't *know* every word. You have given them confidence and high morale.

There are two major benefits of them understanding and communicating in these ways. Firstly, they will talk, they are happy to talk and they enjoy talking. Secondly, they have measured themselves against real English and have developed successful strategies for understanding and communicating. Here are some of the strategies they have developed:

- *Understanding* Watch the speaker's eyes and face. Watch the speaker's gestures. Listen to the speaker's intonation. Look for clues to context, e.g. objects, what the speaker looks at. Guess what they are saying using all this information.
- *Communicating* Use your face. Use gestures. Use intonation. Look at and point to things to help convey context. Make eye contact with your listener.

If they were to go to England or another English-speaking country tomorrow, can you see how they would understand and communicate? They can see now that words are *added* to understanding and to communication. Words help to make communication better, more interesting and more detailed. Words are fun things to use to communicate with. By contrast on some beginner's courses words are

- problems invented to make lessons difficult
- items in tests to get wrong
- things to avoid saying for fear of being wrong.

Keeping the language English

Can your classroom be a little corner of an English-speaking country? As your students step in through the door do they enter a completely English-speaking environment? Here are some ways to help your classroom language to be English. There are 12 ideas and two worked examples.

1. Everyone is visual, verbal or practical, or a mixture of all three, so have in your classroom in each lesson something to *see* (visual), something to *hear* (verbal), something to *touch* or that looks good to touch (practical). For example, as your students walk in there could be a poster of London, a tape playing with an English song they know and an English toy, statuette, bunch of flowers or football scarf.

2. When your students look up (on the walls) or when they look down (on cards in each group) have a *message* there, e.g. 'We speak English here', 'English only', 'English spoken'.

3. Create a specific English-speaking *location*, e.g. 'This is Liverpool. It is the Football Match today between Liverpool and Manchester United'. This could be written or said. The classroom becomes Liverpool and you and all your students become Liverpudlians.

4. Give *rewards* for speaking English, e.g. smile, make eye contact, nod in encouragement and understanding, touch, give praise and applause. Give *'punishments'* for speaking mother tongue, e.g. frown, look away, step back, pretend not to understand.

5. After between 10 and 20 lessons agree a system of *fines* for speaking mother tongue, e.g. coins, matchsticks or slips of paper to put in a box. (You have to pay a fine too if you use their mother tongue.) Agree when in each lesson fines are in force, e.g. 'English only for the next 20 minutes'. At the end of the term have a whole lesson (in English) deciding how the class will spend the money. Then spend it that way, e.g. on an English party.

6. Sometimes the concentration of the class goes and the class becomes chaotic. Then you can insist on *'compulsory talking'* of mother tongue. Stop whatever you were trying to do and get everyone to talk using mother tongue for exactly one minute all together, all at once. At the 59th second yell 'Stop!' Then say 'Can we all speak English for the next nine minutes?' and get on with the lesson.

7. If everyone comes in bubbling with yesterday's local or national news, or there's a fire in the street outside the classroom window, don't fight it, flow with it! Ask them to talk about it in their own language in pairs, then, when the surge of excitement has gone down a bit, ask them to change partners and talk about the event in English.

8. *Become* a new English-speaking teacher who doesn't understand your students' mother tongue at all, e.g. disguise yourself with a hat, scarf or jacket. (You can also put on an accent and get them to interview you before you continue with the lesson as the 'new' teacher. In your answers you can 'sow' what you want to teach next.)

9. In groups the students elect or appoint a *monitor* whose job it is to keep that group speaking English.

10. Go round with a tape recorder and *microphone* recording what your students are saying. (You don't need to play it back or even to have it switched on. The microphone is a reminder.) Or you could appoint a student to go round with the tape recorder and microphone, or just a microphone, or even a cardboard cut-out microphone as a reminder.

11. In groupwork one group volunteers to be a *film crew* (director, camera person, sound person, etc). They can have real or dummy equipment or do it all in mime.

They go round 'filming' the other groups.

12. Make sure the *task* is in English. When your students know that what they have to create or perform (e.g. poem, dialogue or sketch) has to be in English, they use English to create or prepare it. It also helps for each group to have the instructions for the task written in English on a slip of paper.

Worked example 12

Keeping the language English

Lesson aim: To start the lesson with English as the classroom language
Time: 5−10 minutes

1. Have your students relax and sit silently. Say slowly 'You are English or American . . . silently say to yourself your first name as the English or American person that you now are . . . Now say silently your family name . . . So you can say your first name and your family name . . . Where do you live? Is it a village, a town, a city? . . . What part of England or the USA do you live in? . . . So you can say silently your name and where you live . . . What do you do? Do you have a job? What do you do? . . . Silently say your name, where you live and what you do . . . Lastly what are your hobbies or your interests? . . . So you can say silently your name, where you live, what you do, and what your hobbies and your interests are . . .'

2. In pairs students introduce themselves and talk as their new personalities.

3. Change pairs and repeat.

4. Get on with the lesson now everyone *is* an English native speaker.

Worked example 13

Keeping the language English

Lesson aim: To start the lesson with English as the classroom language
Time: 5−15 minutes

Preparation: Have loose pictures of individual people, two for each student. Spread the pictures out on a table

1. The students should divide into pairs. One from each pair chooses a picture, brings it back to show their partner and talks about it.

2. The other person in each pair does the same.

3. You say 'You are becoming that picture. That person is you. Think what your name is . . . Now talk to your partner starting with "I. . ." as if you were the person in the picture'.

4. They change partners and interview each other as if they were the people in the pictures.

5. Get on with the lesson now everyone *is* an English native speaker.

Classroom negotiation language

You set your students some group or pairwork. What do they need to say to one another to negotiate and get the work done? Here are some of the things they might say:

'What did he say? I don't understand. What does this . . . mean? How long have we got? You do it. It's not my turn. You write, I'll think. What do we do next? I've finished, we're finished. We're ready.'

If you teach your students how to say these things *in English*, they will say them in English and English will become the language of classroom negotiation. If you don't teach them how to say these things in English, their mother tongue will dominate in their groupwork.

Worked example 14

Classroom negotiation language

Lesson aim: To teach some classroom negotiation language
Time: 5 minutes

Acknowledgement: Tessa Woodward

1. Say 'OK?'⌣ step to join the class and say 'OK'⌐. Do that twice then get your students to do it with you. Then say 'OK?'⌣ and get your students to reply 'OK'⌐.

2. Now mime that you are not OK, e.g. you don't understand. Say 'No'⌐. Ask 'OK?'⌣ and step to join the class and say 'No'⌐. Say 'OK?'⌣ and your students reply 'No'⌐.

3. Carry on with the lesson using 'OK?'⌝ and getting 'OK' ⌝ or
   'No'   as replies several times at appropriate moments.

4. Next lesson repeat with 'Ready?'⌝ , 'Ready' ⌝, 'No'⌝.

5. Third lesson do the same with 'Finished?'⌝, 'Finished'⌝, 'No'⌝.

After a few lessons of teaching 'OK?' you can add the personal pronoun. It's still natural informal English to say 'You OK?' (reply 'OK'/'No'). Then a few lessons later add the verb 'Are you OK?' (reply 'OK'/'No'). Do the same with 'Ready?' (You ready?', 'Are you ready?') and with 'Finished?' ('You finished?', 'Have you finished?').

See how the intonation carries the meaning and step by step over a few weeks you are adding the grammar to what your students *already understand*. They are hearing the present perfect for the first time when you say 'Have you finished?' and yet they already understand the meaning.

You can then teach the more formal replies such as 'I'm OK', 'I'm OK, thanks', 'We're OK, thank you', 'I'm ready', 'Yes, we're ready', 'Sorry, we're not ready yet', 'I've finished', 'No, we're not finished yet', and so on.

Look again at the paragraph in italics on page 25. See how you could start with English noises or gestures or words.

For example, *'Eh? (What did he say?), Uh? (I don't understand). ... ? (the word repeated with rising intonation — what does .·. mean?) Tap watch and raise eyebrows (How long?) You! (You do it) Not me (It's not my turn) You! (gesture write) I (gesture think) Now? (What do we do next?) Finished. Ready.'*

Work out how you could introduce these in a similar way to Worked Example 14.

Real negotiation is real communication. English can be the natural language for classroom negotiation.

Why not simply translate?

This is one of the arguments where teachers throw coffee cups at one another in the staffroom! Dare I even take sides? I must admit that if I know the word in my students' language and I haven't been able to get them to understand it in English, I do use the translation. But then so few words have a completely equivalent word in another language. The translated word seldom has the same connotation, usage, or figurative or symbolic meanings. I certainly don't want my students getting into the habit of translating every word. And as we've seen, we can help our students through mime, gestures, noises, pictures, objects and actions to have the experience first, and then to put the English word to that experience. In a way we are using the already existing international 'language' (of mime, pictures, etc) which has no words. That's what I am trying to encourage you to do — to think how you could communicate what you want them to learn *without* using their mother tongue at all.

For example, with your beginners in their first few lessons use gestures for instructions instead of mother tongue instructions. Think of gestures for each of these: stand up, sit down, be quiet, listen, close the door, open the windows, look, write, pick up your books, open your books, close your books, work in pairs, make threes, stand up and make a circle and listen, sit down in fours and watch me, talk in threes, think, remember, repeat after me, say it again. Then, in future lessons, use the same gestures but add the words in English. Later you can drop the gestures as they will have learned what the words mean.

If you went to live in a foreign country tomorrow where you didn't know the language, you would use all these strategies. You may translate a few words and phrases in your head to help you grasp them. But most words and phrases you would gradually simply understand from their context and situation through natural language acquisition. And you almost certainly wouldn't open your mouth for 3 months! Yet we expect our beginner students of English to speak in the very first lesson!

That's not very natural or fair. So here I make a plea for silence. Don't pressurise your students to speak. Create opportunities, yes, but if one or two don't want to speak, be patient and leave them until they do. Notice how in the tips and worked examples so far we have suggested that your students listen and understand before they speak. When they do speak, they are not speaking 'in public' to the whole class but speaking just to one person *while* everyone else is speaking. Only when they've gained confidence in private are they asked to speak 'in public'.

Let's go back to imagining you are a beginner in a country and language that is completely foreign to you. You're happy to sing along at a party, or chant along with the crowd. You'll murmur to yourself the words you hear in the bank and the shops. You'll try out new words quietly, to yourself, then aloud in a private situation in a shop or to a friend with nobody else listening. Only then will you use that word to a group of friends, or when lots of people are listening.

I love that moment of breakthrough in a foreign language where I've begun to *think* in that language, and the words just come out. But before that there were months of silent listening and understanding and 'private' experimenting.

TIP: If your students *are* translating every word, speed up your speaking. Give them just enough time to understand the message, but not enough time to translate. Get them to respond (e.g. with an action) immediately to the message. That shows them they can understand *without* translating and it forces them to begin to think in English.

Worked example 15

Why not simply translate?

Lesson aim: To break the habit of translating everything
Time: 5 minutes

1. Speak very fast with no pauses, e.g. 'Stand up. Pick up your book.
    Put down your book. Sit down. Open your book at page one. Close
    your book. Look at the door. Look at the window. Look at me.
    Stand up again. Give your book to your partner. Take it back. Sit
    down. Good!'

2. In pairs each student prepares in their head or writes a series of ten
    such orders. In turn each student orders the other student, speaking
    fast with no pauses.

3. One student volunteers and gives you orders while the others watch.

---

*Listening to rapid, natural speech prepares your students for real English. Increased
speed can decrease translation.*

The classroom with no desks moved

The classroom furniture is important. We're now going to look at ways of working
in the classroom. In the diagrams which follow, these symbols are used:

×	= student
T	= teacher
▭	= desk
×–×	= two students working in a pair
△	= group of three students
O	= centre of a group of four students
→	= movement in one direction
↔	= movement in both directions

This book is full of practical ways of teaching which involve getting your beginners
to talk in pairs, threes, fours and bigger groups. You may have a 'traditional' classroom
with desks or tables in rows and the tables may be fixed to the floor, or you may
not have the time or the permission (or the tolerance and understanding from colleagues)
to move them.

Dominic Parker

Dominic Parker

We will now look at ways your students can work in pairs, and change pairs, and work in threes and fours where it is only the students who turn or move, not the tables or chairs.

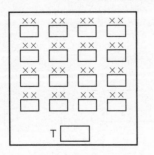

Diagram 7.   A traditional classroom   Diagram 8.   Pairwork

Dominic Parker

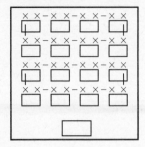

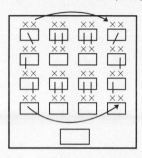

Diagram 9. First change of pairs — nobody moves place

Diagram 10. Second change of pairs — only two students move place

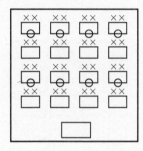

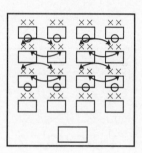

Diagram 11. Fours — nobody moves

Diagram 12. First change of fours — eight students as four pairs swap places

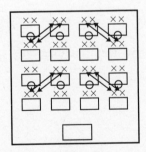

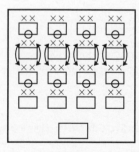

Diagram 13. Second change of fours — pairs swap places

Diagram 14. Third change of pairs — four pairs swap places

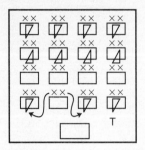

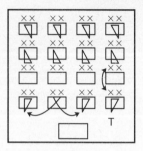

Diagram 15.   Threes — two students move place

Diagram 16.   First change of threes — two students move , two swap

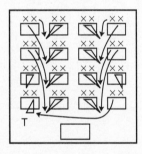

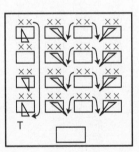

Diagram 17.   Second change of threes — nine students move

Diagram 18.   Third change of threes — nine students move

To get your students to move like this you can show them the diagrams, possibly drawn on a large piece of paper.

The classroom with desks moved

In this section we'll show the classroom with just four desks moved, then we'll look at desk arrangements which are alternatives to rows. It takes only five seconds to move four desks and five seconds to put them back. The effect is to focus the students on themselves instead of the teacher, and it makes a space for standing activities.

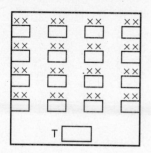

Diagram 19.   The traditional classroom

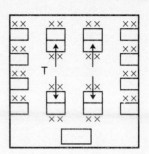

Diagram 20.   With four desks moved; moved students sitting the other side

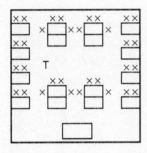

Diagram 21.   Moved students sitting at sides

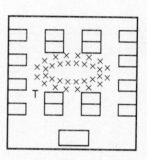

Diagram 22.   Concentric Circles standing close

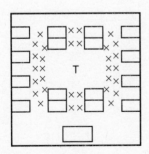

Diagram 23.   Concentric Circles standing wide

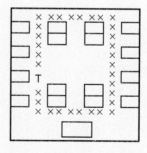

Diagram 24.   Big Circle standing, e.g. Action Chains

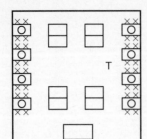

Diagram 25.   Fours sitting

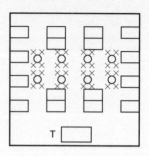

Diagram 26.   Fours standing

In the following diagrams, half the desks are moved. They can be moved and put back in ten seconds in each lesson, or can be left like that. The transformation changes the class emphasis towards groupwork.

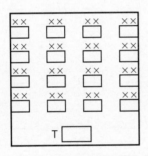

Diagram 27.   The traditional classroom

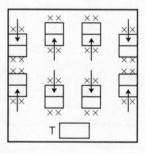

Diagram 28.   Fours across desks, eight desks moved

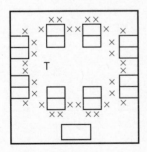

Diagram 29.   Fours around desks (as in Diagram 28)

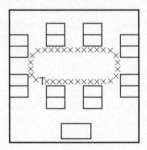

Diagram 30.   Big Circle standing or sitting as in Diagram 28

In the following diagrams, all the desks are put against the walls.

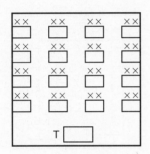

Diagram 31. The traditional classroom

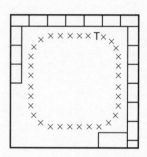

Diagram 32. Big Circle standing or sitting — all desks against the wall

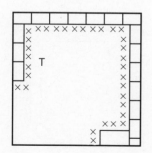

Diagram 33. Pairwork as in Diagram 32

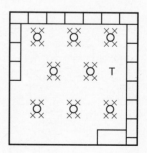

Diagram 34. Fours sitting as in Diagram 32

In the next diagrams, half the desks are against the wall.

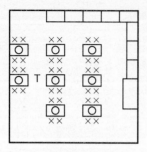

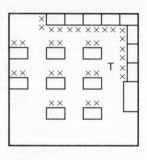

Diagram 35.   Fours

Diagram 36.   Pairwork

In the next diagrams are some horseshoe shapes where the focus is the board but there's still space for groupwork.

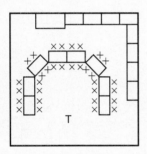

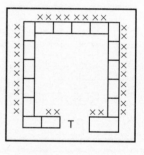

Diagram 37.   Horseshoe with half the desks

Diagram 38.   Square horseshoe with all desks (and pairwork)

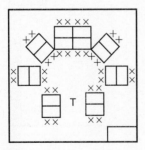

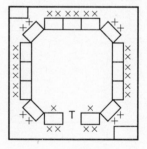

Diagram 39.   Horseshoe with all desks doubled

Diagram 40.   Rounded horseshoe using all but two desks

TIP: Get your students to measure the desks/tables and the classroom and to make a scale drawing of the room. They can then cut out paper scale versions of all the desks and you, or they, can try out the different possible arrangements to decide what would be best. If other colleagues use the room, you now have a scale drawing to show them an arrangement which could help your teaching, and using Diagrams 7 to 40 you can show how easily individual work, pairwork and groupwork can happen.

Practicalities

Students, room, teacher, course book and lessons

In Part One we demonstrated ways of communicating messages first, then adding the words. We saw how the students can work in pairs, groups or various circles so that they communicate together. We saw how your students and the chairs and tables in the classroom can be moved and used to make pairs and groups work better. The examples showed how you, the teacher, can create student-centred lessons which encourage your students to speak without exposing them to embarrassment. We outlined ways of using the course book by finding in this book's indexes the grammar or vocabulary or function which you plan to teach, then using the activities, role-plays, simulations and discussions in Part Two to supplement or substitute for course book lessons.

Activities

The activities are designed to involve your students and motivate them to be interested in the lesson. They are all interactive, making them student-centred and communicative.

There are 39 groups of activities, listed on the contents page, with each group containing three activities: A, B and C. Each group of activities is on a different topic and includes three stages of learning:

- Activity A — these are usually very brief and intended as *warm-ups*, usually starting from what your students know already and getting them to think about the topic or theme of the lesson.

- Activity B — these are *presentations*, designed to let your students hear, see and experience the new grammar and/or functions and/or vocabulary that you want to teach.

- Activity C — these are the initial *practice* stages which are designed to encourage the students to use the new grammar/functions/vocabulary. At this last stage, the students are gaining confidence, experimenting with saying new words and sentences, and assimilating them into their own experience. Some teachers call this stage 'controlled practice'.

Each activity begins with a table showing:

- topic
- words
- grammar
- function
- preparation

for the lesson.

After the table there are instructions for you to follow. Each stage in the lesson sequence is numbered and timings are given for guidance.

The following worked examples show the lay-out and style of the activities. The first worked example shows an Activity A and an Activity B.

Worked example 16: Activities A and B

Topic: The day's routine
Words: Breakfast, lunch, tea/dinner, supper
Grammar: Present simple (habitual) at . . .
Function: Telling the time
Preparation: A large clock with hands that you can move, or large
                  drawings of clocks

A (5 minutes)

1. Set the clock at 7 am. Make ticking noises. Make sleep noises and mime sleep. Make an alarm clock noise and wake and look at the clock. 1 minute.

2. Students brainstorm words they know, e.g. clock, morning, sleep. Write their words and write 7 am or 7 o'clock on the board. 1 minute.

3. Show another time, e.g. 1 pm. Call up a volunteer to mime what they do at that time, e.g. eat lunch. Encourage all the students to make appropriate noises. 1 minute.

4. Repeat step 1, but this time say sentences as you mime, e.g. 'I wake up at 7 am, I get out of bed at 7.10, I wash at 7.11, I make breakfast at 7.30'. 2 minutes.

B (4 minutes)

1. In pairs each student draws a clock showing a particular time and

mimes what they do at that time. You go round putting what they do into words, e.g. 'You put on the television at 6 pm'. 2 minutes.

2. New pairs repeat step 1. You go round again saying the sentences for what they do. 2 minutes

Activity A is a five-minute warm-up which gets your students thinking about times and what they do at different times. It also gets them hearing action words in the present simple with 'at' and a time. Activity A is also your model for your students to follow in Activity B when the students themselves choose the times and the actions to mime. This is student-centred pairwork with the messages clear without words. Within this already communicative activity, you, the teacher, are the resource, going round putting their mimes into words. Activity B is therefore a listening comprehension which your students understand perfectly because they are already doing the actions to which you fit the words. Activity B is therefore a very effective presentation of the new items. (You could have done Activity A already in a previous lesson to 'sow the seeds'.)

The following worked example shows an Activity C which might follow on from the previous Activity A and Activity B.

Worked example 17: Activity C.

C (12 minutes)

1. Make a big circle. Stand in the centre. Going round clockwise say the 12 numbers as they appear on a clock for each member, pointing to the student who is standing in that position. The 12 students take half a step forward. Point again and the 12 students say their numbers. Point again and say 'o'clock' after each number. All the students then say '... o'clock' after the number when you point. Then point randomly at the numbers so the students say '... o'clock'. 2 minutes.

2. Gather the students on either side of each numbered student into groups. Ask them to prepare a mime for what they do at that time. You go round putting words to their mimes. 3 minutes.

3. You stand behind each group to prompt them. Each group in turn (clockwise) presents their mime and says their sentence(s). Then each group presents their mime again and *all* the students say that sentence, e.g. 'At 8 o'clock I travel to school'. 7 minutes.

Activity C is *controlled practice* first as mime, then with sentences in groups, then finally with everyone saying each sentence. Your students are then ready to use these new language items more freely and you can use them in the role-plays, simulations and discussions which follow the activity. But first let's look at how to choose an activity.

Students listen well when they are already doing what the words describe.

How to choose an activity for its usefulness

If we look at Activities A, B and C above, you could use A, then B, then C. Or you could use only one of them. Or you could use A+B, B+C or A+C.

If the unit in the course book you use is already quite student-centred, you could use A as a warm-up *supplement* and then move on to the course book. If the course book is trying to get your students to talk about the characters in the course book and your students don't relate to them or are having difficulty because they are bored with them, you could use A+B+C to *substitute* for the course book lesson. If the course book material (content) is good, but the method or activity (process) in the course book is not so good, you could use the techniques in this book as *processes to deliver the content* you choose.

For example, if your course book has an activity to teach five new words and you think the activity given is not sufficiently student-centred, you might decide to use an Action Chain to teach the five new words from the course book. That is an example of you using a *process* from this book to deliver the *content* you choose from the course book.

TIP: This means that you can also use an activity from this book to teach grammar, functions and vocabulary other than those that the activity has been designed for.

A dynamic activity can be adapted to 'deliver' different content.

How to choose an activity to suit your style

Some teachers say 'A teacher must be an actor.' I don't agree. Many excellent teachers have teaching styles which are quiet and not at all extrovert. What is your style? If you prefer *not* to act or mime or tell stories, I guarantee there will be a student in your class who will gladly do these for you. Nowadays I do very little 'acting' in the classroom. I get my students to do it for me.

TIP: If you prefer, you can plan your activities so that an extrovert student does what this book says for the teacher to do. You can stand behind the student and whisper instructions as to what to do, and whisper the words that student should say. (You can even be holding this book in your hand and reading it while you instruct!)

So, what style have you chosen as appropriate for a particular lesson? Choose the activity that fits in best with your plan.

In the next section we will look at role-plays, simulations and discussions.

Role-plays, simulations and discussions

We are using the following definitions:

- In a *role-play* each student pretends to be someone else and does something which has been set for them to do.

- In a *simulation* each student *is* himself or herself and does something which has been set for them to do.

- In a *discussion* each student is himself or herself and does what comes naturally.

We'll put it another way. In role-play you *are not* yourself. In simulation and discussion you *are* yourself. In role-play and simulation you say what the *teacher guides* you to say. In discussion you say what *you want* to say. Role-play is *created* and *controlled*. Simulation is *controlled*. Discussion is *free*.

The following diagrams show this in graphic form.

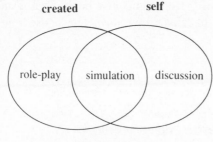

Diagram 41.

Artificial	'Authentic'	Real
role-play	simulation	discussion
other person	me	me
other ideas	other ideas	my ideas

Diagram 42.

This is the ideal progression for getting your students to talk. First, in role-play your students are practising the new items (grammar, function, vocabulary) at two removes. In simulation they are practising at one remove. In discussion they are expressing themselves directly. The advantage of moving through these three stages is that your students have repeated the new items several times before they use the new items for their own purposes. Let's look at an analogy to explain this further.

You want to buy a car. You imagine what it would be like and you sit in a chair and pretend you are driving it (role-play). Then you go to a garage and sit in the real car you fancy, and you try out all the levers, knobs, switches etc and adjust the seat (simulation). Then you really start it up and go for a test drive (discussion). Only after actually test driving the real car are you sufficiently confident in the future to step into any car of that make and model and drive wherever you want to go. It's easier to drive if you pretend first and gain confidence by sitting in a car and 'getting the feel' of it, and waiting until your confidence has grown enough to start the engine and drive off.

So, in this book we progress in each lesson from role-play to simulation to discussion. In this way your students will become very willing to talk because, step by step, situations will become more real and personal.

Gradually ease your students into personal reality.

Why use role-plays, simulations and discussions?

We've looked at the principle of easing students gradually into the 'personal' and the 'real'. If they are going to mumble and fumble and get things wrong, it's better that they do it where it is not their real selves being incompetent, and it is not what they, personally, want to say that is coming out wrong. In this way role-play protects your students' inner selves from suffering any blows to their confidence and morale while getting to use the new items of language. As they gain in competence and when they are making fewer errors, you can move them into simulation. In simulation, they are being themselves, but they are not speaking 'from the heart' yet, so they and their listeners are still very tolerant of hesitations and errors. When they are gaining in fluency in the new items, and are ready to be themselves *and* to speak from the heart, you can move them into discussion.

Give the students opportunities to be fluent first before they speak as themselves for themselves.

You could of course stop as soon as your students are able to say the new words and not bother with role-plays, simulations and discussions. The activities in this book are designed to teach each new item, following the natural sequence of learning. In the first activities your students learn passively (listen and understand). In the next stage the students learn actively (speak). In the final stage the students practise the new items. You could stop at that final stage, and if you pressed the same switch again (e.g. the cue word) your students would be able to say the new words. If you pressed that switch in a test, they might even get full marks. But what of your aim to prepare your students to use the new words in the outside world? What if the people in the real world who meet your students don't give your students the same cue word?

To avoid confusion and uncertainty in the real outside world, we need to push the new words to a greater depth of learning. We need to involve the students' creativity and imagination in using the words. We need them to use the new words to communicate, to express themselves, and to talk about their own feelings and experiences. Only then will the new words have been fully integrated into their lives. Such fully integrated words are ready to be used at any time in the real outside world and need no trigger or cue.

Diagram 43.   Layers of learning a new word 'to a greater depth of learning'

This book	Teacher speaking	Student learning	The lesson	
			The skills	The stages
First activity	communicating the meaning (not saying the word)	understanding the message	listening	warm-up
Second activity	saying the word saying the word in a sentence	understanding the word understanding the word in context responding appropriately not saying the word	listening	presentation
Third activity	saying the word in other sentences too	saying the word responding appropriately saying the word	pronunciation speaking	pronunciation
Fourth activity	using the word in a freer context	saying the word in a sentence in a situation	speaking	controlled practice
Role-play		saying the word in a sentence in a second situation using the word to communicate	role-play* speaking	further practice
Simulation		saying the word in a sentence in a third situation using the word to communicate as self	simulation* speaking	further practice
Discussion		saying the word in a sentence using the word to communicate as self about self	discussion* speaking	free stage

* including writing and reading when required.

Students should practise and explore a new word until it fully integrates with their lives.

Layers of learning

The concept of layers of learning is illustrated in Diagram 43.

You can see how little the teacher needs to speak, and how the burden of work shifts from the teacher to the students very early on. The teacher is freed to manage the lesson, to set the activities, role-plays, simulations and discussions, to supervise, to be a resource, and to be a real person for the students to communicate with.

Some people express these extra depths of learning in terms of using the different parts of the brain one by one until the new word and its meaning, responses, associations, feelings and connotations are all experienced. The word is then 'in the brain' as a whole.

A brain is not really so divided, but is an integrated whole. However some people believe there are specialisms in each half and Diagram 44 shows how this book's methods help to use the *whole brain*.

Diagram 44   Right brain, left brain, whole brain

Left brain	Right brain
Left brain qualities	**Right brain qualities**
Logical, verbal, linear, reality-based	Intuitive, non-verbal, holistic, fantasy-oriented
Symbolic, sequential, temporal, abstract	Concrete, random, non-temporal, analogic
Specialisms	**Specialisms**
Language, reading, writing	Feelings and emotions
Listening, auditory association	Visualisation, art expression
Talking and reciting, phonics	Creativity, colour sensitivity
Following directions, symbols	Music and singing, shapes, patterns
Locating details and facts	Spatial relationships, body awareness
Getting beginners to talk	
Understand noises and words ⟶	Understand mime, body language
+Understand meaning in activity ⟵	+Respond non-verbally in activity
+Respond verbally in activity ⟵	+Physical activity, senses
+Verbal imagination in role-play ⟵	+Non-verbal imagination in role-play
+Logic in simulation ⟵	+Emotion in simulation
+Reason in discussion ⟵	+Feelings in discussion
Whole brain	

In this book we are trying to use the right brain as much as the left by creating at least ten crossovers per lesson. In this way each student is helped to use their whole brain very thoroughly. Both right-brain dominant students and left-brain dominant students are equally well-served and will learn equally well from the way you teach.

What are you? Look again at the qualities and specialisms and see if you are better with left-brain or right-brain items. Look again and decide where your teaching style lies. You may even want to look at where your course book fits in with your style.

The idea of right and left brains may well be proved to be merely a creation of scientists. It is still a useful symbol, however, for discussing different students' strengths and weaknesses. The different specialisms in Diagram 44 are important to cater for whether they are on only one side of the brain or not.

Teach using all the various different strengths of all the different students.

How to choose role-plays, simulations and discussions

If your students already know the new items you have taught (e.g. grammar, function, vocabulary) you can use a role-play, simulation or discussion as an oral stage or revision. If they are already very confident, they can go straight to a discussion (after a warm-up to get them interested in the topic). If your students are only just beginning to use the new items for the first time, then it is best to move from the activities step by step through a role-play and simulation before having a discussion. Your students' mood and interest may be the deciding factors. They may prefer the role-play to the simulation or a discussion if they want to be other people and want to use their imagination and creativity. On the other hand, they may be longing to express what they themselves think and would therefore prefer a simulation or discussion to a role-play. It could be that a discussion fits most accurately with what your students are interested in or want to express. Or it could be a role-play or simulation. Feel free to use only one, or all three to suit your particular students and that particular lesson.

> TIP: If the role-play really 'takes off', let it run on longer. Forget the simulation and discussion, or use them for revision a few weeks later.

Summary

Here's a summary of the advice given so far. You, the teacher, are the expert on your class and your course book. You know your students, what they have done and haven't done, what they can and can't do, what they like and don't like. You, the teacher, are also the expert on the course book you use. So you might use one activity from this book as a one minute warm-up at the start of your course book lesson, and you might use just the five minute discussion from this book as the free practice at the end of your course book lesson. Or you might put aside the course book completely and use this book for your whole lesson. Alternatively, you could do something in between these two extremes. If you've 'sown the seeds' of a new item, your students can move through the processes in a lesson very fast. You can even skip stages and do two activities and go straight to the discussion.

When your students are learning fast you can speed up your teaching.

Here are some last minute tips on using the activities, role-plays, simulations and discussions.

1. Get your students to correct themselves. If they can't, get other students to correct them. Only if they can't, correct the student yourself.

2. When you set your students an activity, role-play, simulation or discussion, there is usually a period of silence or random talking or movement as they adjust themselves to what they are about to do. *Don't step into that silence.* Sit down. Sit back. Look away. Then your message to your students is 'You get on with it. You *can* do it'. (If you stand up and look anxious they all look at you expecting you to do all the work for them!)

3. Beware of simplifying the ideas when you simplify the language! For example a student can communicate real, complex emotions with gesture and face. If you only accept words such as 'happy' and 'sad', you are treating the students as superficial. Why not, instead, accept a mixture of face, gesture and words — some emotions communicated silently, others also with words?

4. When planning a lesson ask yourself 'Would this lesson be interesting for an English native speaker of the same age and character as my students?' If the answer is 'no', then that lesson may be intrinsically uninteresting and therefore may not involve or motivate your students. Perhaps you need to add challenges to your students to use their intelligence and experience so they are working as complete people and not only as learners.

5. Ask yourself 'Will I enjoy this lesson? Will I learn something interesting?' If the answer is 'no', how can *you* be motivated? Maybe you need to incorporate more challenge for *you*.

6. *You* are important. Your interests, your personal and professional rewards and satisfactions from the job are important. Your desire to develop and grow as a teacher is important. Value yourself.

PART TWO

ACTIVITIES, ROLE-PLAYS, SIMULATIONS AND DISCUSSIONS

Activity 1   I like, I don't like

Topic:	Likes and dislikes 1
Words:	TV, video, computer, Coca Cola, hamburger, Michael Jackson, Big Ben, punk, rock and roll, Sony Walkman, pop music (to famous people in the news, popular groups), I like, I don't like
Grammar:	I like, I don't like
Function:	Expressing likes and dislikes
Preparation:	Six or more colourful pictures of international themes: well-known people or places, etc.

A   International words (8 minutes)

1. Write 'English' on the board. Write 'OK' on the board. Point to other spaces and silently encourage your students to give you 20 or 30 more international words. Say the words they give you. You write some as well, e.g. football, London. Draw a heart ♡ . Put your hands on your heart and say 'Mm Michael Jackson' (if you like Michael Jackson) or 'Mm football' (if you like football).

2. Draw another heart and cross it out ⊗ . Make a rejecting gesture say 'Nn hamburger' (if you don't like hamburgers) or 'Nn Coca Cola' (if you don't like Coca Cola).

3. Put your students into pairs. They gesture to each other 'Mm' or 'Nn' communicating their likes and dislikes. Go round communicating more of your own likes and dislikes. Then next to ♡ write 'I like' and say it. Next to ⊗ write 'I don't like' and say it. Now say 'I like Michael Jackson. I don't like hamburgers. I like football, I don't like Coca Cola'.

4. Your students then say their likes and dislikes.

B   Loan words (5 minutes)

1. In English there will be some words from your students' mother tongue(s). Collect

a list of the 10 most useful ones and remember them. (The spelling and pronunciation may be different but they will still be recognisable.) Add these words one by one to the international words and say them in a very English way. Now get your students to change partners and say 'I like . . .' and 'I don't like . . .' about those words too. (If there are very few loan words, add some more international words.)

C   International pictures (8 minutes)

1. Have six or more pictures ready. They should be pictures your students will recognise immediately, and for which there are international or loan words, e.g. Prince Charles, Big Ben. Show the pictures and say the words after your students have said them. Stick the pictures on the board, point to the pictures again to get the students to say the words again. Write the words on the board.
2. Your students can then change partners and say 'I like . . .' and 'I don't like . . .' about the pictures. Then they can all walk round saying to each person they meet 'I like . . .' or 'I don't like . . .'.
3. Have your students stand in a circle. You say 'I like . . .'. Go quickly round the circle with each student saying 'I like . . .'. You say 'I don't like . . .'. Go quickly round the circle with each student saying 'I don't like . . .'.
4. The students could think of more international and loan words for their homework and bring them to the next lesson.

If possible, use big sheets of paper for this activity so you can use the work in role-play 2.

Role-play, simulation and discussion 1

Topic: Likes and dislikes 1

Words: (see Activity 1) + you, he, she, do, does, doesn't, no, yes

Grammar: I like, I don't like
you like, you don't like
he likes, she likes, he doesn't like, she doesn't like
Do you like? No. Yes

Function: Asking about likes/dislikes. We like, we don't like

Preparation: Pictures and name cards

Role-play 1: Interviews of famous people (10 minutes)

1. Choose the name or picture of an internationally known person from the board (see Activity 1C). You say 'I am ... I like ... I don't like ... I like ... I don't like ...'.
2. Have ready enough international names or names plus pictures so that there is one for each pair of students. Lay them face down. One student from each pair chooses one name or picture. In pairs, the student shows the name or picture to their partner and says 'I am ... I like ... I don't like ...'. The students can then swap cards in their pair and change pairs so they have one card per pair. Repeat the last exercise with the new pairs.
3. Choose a name or picture. Don't show it. Say 'I like ... I don't like ... I like ... I don't like ... I am?' Your students try to guess. You show the picture/name after three guesses and say 'I am ...'.
4. Your students then give the cards in. You shuffle them. The students choose one card for each new pair. They imitate what you have just done and you go round saying 'You are ... You are ...' when they have said 'I am ...'.
5. Choose one student. Get her or him to choose a card. You don't look at it. You say 'Do you like ...? Do you like ...? Don't you like ...?' etc. Show that student how to say 'yes' and 'no'. You then guess 'You are ...'. After three guesses the student shows the card.

6.   Your students make new pairs and with new cards one interviews the other as that famous person. Then they swap and change pairs so that the interviewer becomes the interviewee.

Simulation 1: Interviews of themselves (10 minutes)

1.   Collect the cards in from the role-play. Your students split into threes (A, B and C). They are themselves. A interviews B. C notes or remembers B's answers (e.g. A 'Do you like . . .?' B 'yes/no'). After ten or so questions C reports 'You like . . . you don't like . . .' etc.
2.   Next, C interviews A while B notes, then B interviews C and A notes.
3.   Now all your students stand or sit in a circle. Each student is reported on in turn. First you demonstrate. 'Maria likes . . . she doesn't like . . . she likes . . . she doesn't like . . .'. Then your students report on each other. (Two students in each group of three should know the facts about the other students.)

Discussion 1 (10 minutes)

1.   Ask the whole class 'Do you like . . .?'. When you find something which everyone likes, put it at the top of a list. Ask 'Do you like . . .?' trying to find something nobody likes. Put it at the bottom of the list. Make squares for 10 items.
2.   In new groups of three, get your students to prepare a similar list (remembered or written) which is true for them as a group of three, putting their agreed likes in order at the top of the list, non-agreed (likes *and* don't likes) middle of the list, and agreed 'don't likes' at the bottom of the list.
3.   When the first group of three is ready they go around reporting to other threes. You demonstrate with them 'We like . . . we don't like . . .'.

   While the students are working in groups you can go round encouraging them, correcting them (e.g. by whispering the correction into the ear of the one who makes the error you hear), and demonstrating again if needed through communicating about yourself.

Activity 2 Does he like...?
Does she like...?

Topic: Likes and dislikes 2

Words: Fan club, McDonald's, New York, astronaut, bus,
telephone, radio, I love you, news, pop video,
movie/cinema, cheers!, happy birthday, yellow submarine,
discotheque

Grammar: But ... not, Does he like?, Does she like?, personal
pronouns

Function: Expressing and contrasting likes and dislikes

Preparation: Loan words on cards. Pictures

A More international words (10 minutes)

1. Write 'English' on the board. Slowly write and say some more (about 12)
international words, and encourage your students to add any more (e.g. have a
student standing with you writing what the other students say). Particularly choose
words from song titles or words from songs that you know your students know.
Add some names of pop groups which you know/guess they like and dislike. Ask
'Do you like ...?' a few times.
2. In pairs each student interviews their partner in turn, 'Do you like ...?'. Then
they combine to make fours and your model 'He/she likes ...' so that each student
in turn is reporting on their partner to the other pair.

*You can save the international words for role-plays by writing them on a large piece
of paper or not wiping them off the board.*

B More loan words (10 minutes) (Action Chain)

1. Have ready about 10 words which are words in both your students' language and
in English. (The spelling and pronunciation should not be too different.) Write
each word on a separate card.

55

2. Make a circle, standing, and simply pass each word one by one to your right. This stage is silent. When the first word comes back to you, say it and pass it on, encouraging your students to say each word as they pass it on.
3. When the first word comes back to you the second time, say what is true of your 'I like/I don't like . . .'. Try to make sure your students are each saying what is true of them, then collect all the word cards as they come back to you.
4. Now demonstrate with two students. You are A, they are B and C.
    A: with word card, 'I like . . .'. B to C: 'He/she likes . . . Do you like?'. C to B: 'Yes/no'. You can then continue around the circle as follows. C to D: 'I like . . .'. D to E: 'He/she likes . . .' and so on. As soon as one card is with D, you start with another card. Collect all the word cards as they come back to you.

You can save the loan words for role-plays by writing them on a large piece of paper or not wiping them off the board.

C More pictures (5 minutes)

1. Have ready six more pictures (cut from newspapers or magazines) e.g. of film stars or pop stars your students will all know. Two or three should be ones you like, and two or three ones you don't like. Put the pictures one by one where all your students can all see them, e.g. stuck on the board/laid on a table/spread on the floor. Then point to each in turn and let your students say them.
2. Now say (using very *English* pronunciation of the names and pointing) 'I like . . . but I don't like . . .'. Send one student out of the room (or get them to block their ears) and then say about each of the rest of the pictures 'I like . . . but I don't like . . .'. Bring in the student. The class have to point to each picture and say about you 'She/he likes . . . but she/he doesn't like . . .'.

Role-play, simulation and discussion 2

Topic: Likes and dislikes 2

Words: (see Activity 2) + not, they, name, address, age, number, hobbies, interests, date, signed, who

Grammar: They like, they don't like, we like, we don't like

Function: Giving personal details

Preparation: Forms copied

Role-play 2: Interviews of people of different ages (8 minutes)

1. Use all the words and word cards and pictures from Activity 1A, 1B and 1C, Role-play 1, and Activity 2A, 2B and 2C. Put them where everyone can see them.
2. Have three two-sided picture cards as follows:
   - an old man with an old woman on the other side
   - a 25-year-old woman with a 35-year-old man on the other side
   - a 5-year-old girl with a 5-year-old boy on the other side.
3. The students form groups of three. In their threes they choose one student to be an old man/old woman, one to be a man/woman, and one to be a young boy/girl.
4. It is a free three person interview. 'Do you like . . .?' 'I like . . .' 'He/she likes . . .' 'Does he/she like . . .?' 'I like . . . but I don't like . . .'. You go round interrupting each group asking questions, and making statements about yourself and the students.
5. After three minutes all the old people go to make one group, all the 35-year-olds another, and all the 5-year-olds another. They continue to ask questions and make statements. You go into each group and point to another group and you say 'They like . . . but they don't like . . .' several times. You then go into each group and say, with a gesture including all in that group, 'We like . . . but we don't like . . .' (whatever is true about that group) several times.

Simulation 2: Personal details (5–10 minutes)

1. Each student needs a copy of the form overleaf. The students could copy it from

an overhead projector or from a large piece of paper which you could put on the board. Fill in a version with your details talking as you do it. Translate if necessary. Then ask your students to fill in the form.

Name .... Age ..... Date of birth ....

Address ....

....

Telephone number ....

Hobbies/interests ....

....

Date .... Signed ....

Discussion 2: Find someone who (10 minutes)

1. Each student needs a copy of the form below. The students could copy it from an overhead projector or from a large piece of paper which you could put on the board. Then they all walk round asking the questions they need to ask in order to collect six different names. If necessary you model the first one, e.g. 'Do you like pop music? Do you like rock music?'

Find someone who:

1. Likes pop music but not rock music ....

2. Likes Michael Jackson but not George Michael ....

3. Likes football but not basketball ....

4. Likes television and video and discotheques ....

5. Doesn't like the telephone ....

6. Doesn't like computers and doesn't like Coca Cola ....

---

2. When everyone has six different names, sit down together. You say 'Who doesn't like rock music but does like pop music?' and so on, until you have feedback for all six questions.

Activity 3 Rainbow

Topic: Colours

Words: Colours

Grammar: This is ... that is ... that's ...

Function: Describing, naming colours

Preparation: Prepare pictures and objects of different colours

A   Colours (5 minutes) (Action Chain)

1. Have ready three different things which are red, e.g. red coloured pen, red piece of cloth, red cards; three different things which are white; and so on for all the colours you want to teach.
2. Silently pass the first red thing to the first student who then passes it on to the next student. Pass the second red thing to the first student and say 'red'. The first student says 'red' and passes it on to the second student. Pass the third red thing to the first student and say 'red'. The student says 'red' and passes it on. Do the same routine for the rest of the colours. When the first red thing comes back to you at the end of the chain, send it around in the same direction, saying 'red'. When the second and third objects come back to you, hold on to them and send the first thing for the next colour round saying the colour.
3. Continue until all the things that have gone round silently have their words. Now send all the things round both ways with the words so that there are lots of things and words crossing in both directions.
4. Ask for the things back, pointing to the object, e.g. 'The red pen please. Thank you. The red card ...', etc. (You are *not* teaching these words, just letting your students hear 'red' etc among other words.)

B   Touch blue! (1 minute), Rainbow (3 minutes)

1. Your students stand as a group (or groups of six) close together (you may need separate male and female groups depending on the culture as they may not feel comfortable about touching someone of the opposite sex).
2. Explain in their language or by mime that when you say 'Touch blue' each person

must touch something blue on *someone else*. Do this *very quickly* saying each colour you have taught two or three times, e.g. 'Touch blue ... touch red ... touch green ... touch red ... touch black ... touch white ... touch blue ... touch green ... touch black ... touch white ...'.

3. Draw the shape of a rainbow (with sun and rain) but *without* the seven colours. Your students try to remember and say the colours and you point and they say 'yes' or 'no' as to where the colours are (red orange yellow green blue indigo violet). When they get one right, you write the word in the correct place.

C 'After image' (5 minutes), Flags (5 minutes)

1. Write on the board the names of the colours learned so that after each word there is space to write the colour of the 'after image'. Each student is given something in a particular colour and stares at it for one minute against a background of white (e.g. paper). Then they move the thing and continue to stare at the blank white paper and say what colour they see. (This is the complementary or opposite colour which shows up as the after image.) You write each after image colour on the list next to the image colour.

2. Have or draw a simple map including eight or ten countries your students all know. Have or draw one flag of one country they know. They name the colours. They then have to try to tell you the colours of the flags of the other countries.

Role-play, simulation and discussion 3

Topic: Colours

Words: (See Activity 3) + colour, colours, favourite

Grammar: What . . . do you like? What's your favourite . . .?

Function: Interviewing, agreeing, disagreeing

Preparation: Pictures of stars. Copy forms

Role-play 3: Star interview (5 minutes)

1. From Activity 1 and 2 have pictures of pop or film stars. Choose one student. Give them a choice of three stars. You then interview them, writing the star's name and the answers on a copy of the form shown below reproduced on a large sheet of paper or an overhead transparency. 'What music do you like? . . . What rock groups do you like? . . . What colours do you like?'
2. Now each student in turn becomes a star who is interviewed by three other students. When everyone is finished you ask two students (by their star name) 'What's your favourite colour?'

Name	Name	Name . . . .
Likes music	Favourite music	Favourite music . . . .
. . . .	. . . .	. . . .
Likes pop groups	Favourite pop groups	Favourite pop groups
. . . .	. . . .	. . . .
Likes colours	Favourite colours . . .	Favourite colours . . .
. . . .	. . . .	

Simulation 3: Interview (5 minutes)

1. Use the form from Simulation 2. Ask the students to make pairs. Each student in the pair swaps forms and writes 'Favourite' on the form and interviews their partner by asking 'What's your favourite colour?', 'What's your favourite pop group?', etc. They then note the answers on the form and give the form back to the other student.

Discussion 3: Paint the classroom (10 minutes) (Pyramid Discussion)

1. Divide the students into groups of three. Ask the groups to decide what colour(s) to repaint the classroom. They can draw a quick plan to show their colour scheme.

    *   In sixes, two groups of three argue/agree/compromise and draw their agreed design.
    *   In twelves, two groups of six argue/agree/compromise and draw their agreed design.
    *   In twenty-fours, two groups of twelve argue/agree/compromise and draw their agreed design.

2. For homework, each student could design and draw a flag for the class as a group. They could then show it to the rest of the class and talk about it.

Activity 4 Window

Topic: View from the 'window'

Words: Any in the pictures

Grammar: Here, there

Function: Describing

Preparation: Find two big and detailed pictures (A3 or poster size). You
                    can project a photographic slide if you have one. Place the
                    picture in a position which means that the students can't
                    see it from where they are sitting but can see it when they
                    come up and look (e.g. on a table masked by books/on the
                    floor/behind an upturned table/in a suitcase).

A   Drawing 1st picture (5–10 minutes)

1. Divide the students into groups of three (A, B and C) and make sure each group
    has a piece of paper and a pen/pencil. The entire exercise is to be done silently
    using *gestures only*. As and Bs go up and look at the first picture once for 10
    seconds only. They go back and begin to draw it together. Whenever they are
    uncertain they can send C up to check and tell them what they have forgotten
    or are doing wrong, *but everyone has to be totally silent all the time*. 5 minutes
2. Each group holds up their picture. You hold up your picture. You point and name
    the things in your picture and they point and name the things in theirs.

B   Drawing 2nd picture (5 minutes)

1. Divide the students into pairs (A and B). Each pair has a piece of paper and a
    pen/pencil. As come up and look at the second picture and go back and tell Bs
    what to draw (you are at the picture helping with vocabulary). As can come up
    as often as they like.

C   Drawing in pairs (10–15 minutes)

1. In new pairs A instructs B and B instructs A at the same time. They are each

drawing what they are told but what they are being told is a *mixture* of the things in the first and second pictures. 5–10 minutes

2. Each student holds up their picture, you hold up (or prop up) the first and second pictures and point and name while they point and name and enjoy the mixtures, showing one another. 5 minutes

Role-play, simulation and discussion 4

Topic: Views

Words: Any in the scenes

Grammar: I can see a/some. What can you see? There is, there are. Present simple

Function: Describing

Acknowledgement: Paul Fagg

Role-play 4: Imaginary scenes (10 minutes)

1. In pairs A imagines a scene and guides B as she or he walks through the scene. B (with eyes closed if possible) walks and turns as told by A who also tells B what B can 'see'. B can ask questions. 4 minutes
2. B imagines and A walks. 4 minutes
3. The class gives feedback on their experience in small groups. 2 minutes

Simulation 4: A guided tour (14 minutes)

1. In new pairs A guides B (who is 'blind') through A's own house/flat/room/garden saying what is where. B can ask questions. 4 minutes
2. B guides A. 4 minutes
3. The pairs combine into fours and each student tells the others what they can remember of their partner's house/flat/room/garden. 6 minutes

Discussion 4: An ideal place (10–20 minutes)

1. In threes or fives each group discusses and agrees on their ideal house/flat/room/garden and one or more in each group draws it while talking. 5–10 minutes
2. In sixes or tens they show and discuss the differences and further ideas. 5–10 minutes

Activity 5 Science fiction

Topic: Science fiction robots

Words: Any from pictures and science fiction

Grammar: Past simple in story-telling

Function: Story-telling, narration

Preparation: Science fiction pictures, e.g. book covers or posters or video covers or videos

A Vocabulary (3 minutes)

1. Write on the board two or three science fiction words your students already know (e.g. computer, robot, 2001, Star Wars, spaceship, UFO, time machine, Back to the Future, android etc). Invite your students to brainstorm further science fiction vocabulary. 2 minutes
2. Show the pictures and brainstorm some more. 1 minute

B Drawing a scene (20–25 minutes)

1. In self-selected pairs, ask the students to draw a science fiction scene and encourage them to prepare to talk about it. 5–10 minutes
2. The pairs make sixes and each shows their scene and talks about it. 5 minutes
3. The pairs make new fours and have to make their two scenes into one story to tell. 5 minutes
4. The fours go round to other fours showing their scenes and telling their stories. 5 minutes

C Drawing a story (15–35 minutes)

1. In twos, threes or individually (the students choose), they make up a science fiction story (e.g. completing it for homework). 10–20 minutes
2. The students tell, write or draw and display their stories to one or more other groups. 5–15 minutes

Role-play, simulation and discussion 5

Topic: Travel, technology

Words: Travel and technology, descriptions of places

Grammar: I am, I like, present simple question and answer . . . are/is better because . . .

Function: Interviewing

Role-play 5: Interview (15–25 minutes)

1. After doing Activity 5C each student decides they are a particular character (from their own story or another group's story or from a pubished story or film). They prepare to be interviewed thinking of the likely questions and their answers. 5 minutes
2. In groups of three, each student is interviewed by the other two. 5–10 minutes
3. In new groups of three each *is* their character as interviewer and interviewee. 5–10 minutes

Simulation 5: The experience (8 minutes)

1. Each student is himself/herself but has travelled (e.g. in a time machine) into a science fiction story (e.g. their own, another student's, a published story or film). Each prepares to talk about what it is like to be there and what they do. 5 minutes
2. In groups of three each student talks about the experience. The other two can ask questions.

Discussion 5: The future (20–35 minutes)

1. The students divide into different groups of three (A, B and C). Each group is given a different topic to prepare to talk about (e.g. computers are better than brains; robots are better than people; technology will end the world; machines will control humans; animals will rule the world; the past is better than the future; science is bad; war is always with us; we need enemies). 5 minutes
2. Each A goes to a different group as does each B and C and the new threes combine to make sixes. Each six discusses 'the future'. 5–10 minutes
3. Each six reports to the class on the future as they see it. 10–20 minutes

Activity 6 Letters make words

Topic: The alphabet

Words: Revision, numbers, letters

Grammar: 'Will' future

Function: Predicting, counting, spelling

Preparation: Copy of typewriter keyboard

A   Making words (7 minutes)

1. Write up two vowels and five consonants on the board, e.g. e a s t p c b. In pairs the students write as many English words as they can in three minutes using only those letters (but using them more than once in each word if they need to). You circulate during this time.
2. Choose the pair with the least words to say the words they have made, then invite the class to shout out further words. 2 minutes
3. The pair with the most words chooses the next two vowels and five consonants for a further round but with a two-minute time limit.

B   Further words (7 minutes)

1. In the same pairs the students return to their list of words from Activity 6A. The pairs combine into fours and each pair predicts how many more words the other pair will be able to make when they give them one more letter (to add to the two vowels and five consonants they already have). Each pair gives the other pair the specific extra letter and each pair has three minutes in which to make as many extra words as they can.
2. In their fours the pairs count the extra words they have made and compare them with the predictions. 2 minutes
3. The class discusses the predictions and the usefulness of particular letters. 2 minutes

C   Qwerty (21 minutes)

1. For this activity you will need a typewriter or computer keyboard, or a picture of one.
2. Draw a blank keyboard, i.e. three rows of eight or nine letters. In groups of three the students copy the blank keyboard and try to remember and/or predict and write which letters are on which keys. 5 minutes
3. Add a top row to your drawing. Your students copy that and write on the symbols they remember/predict are on it. 1 minute
4. Now have the real keyboard/picture where only you can see it. One member from each group of three comes up (all at the same time) to look at the keyboard and to go back and tell their group the right answers. 3 minutes
5. Show the keyboard to everybody. (They can count how many they got right.) 1 minute
6. Each group finds a text (e.g. an article in a newspaper, a page in the course book). They organise themselves within their group to discover which six letters are most common with what frequency per 100 letters. 6 minutes
7. The whole class compares results. 3 minutes
8. Each individual has two minutes to make as many words as possible from the agreed six most common letters.

Role-play simulation and discussion 6

Topic: The alphabet

Words: Revision

Grammar: Word order in sentences

Function: Spelling, conversation on a topic

Role-play 6: Favourite letters (7 minutes)

1. Each student writes out the alphabet and then chooses the six letters they like best. They make as many words as they can in two minutes from those letters. 3 minutes
2. In groups of three the students start a conversation. In their conversation, each student has to try to say his/her words. When they say a word on their list, they tick it off. The first to say all his/her words wins. The other two keep playing until the second one has said all his/her words. All three then prepare to say the third student's remaining words in one sentence. 2 minutes
3. Each group says their sentence to the rest of the class. 2 minutes

Simulation 6: My words (5 minutes)

1. Each student writes 20 words they want to use in conversation. 2 minutes
2. In groups of three they have a conversation and, as in the role-play, each student tries to use up all their words. 3 minutes

Discussion 6: The words they need (13 minutes)

1. In new groups of three each group prepares a topic and a list of 30–40 words that will be useful. They write the list on a large piece of paper. 5 minutes
2. The groups of three combine to make six and each three states their topic for discussion, and displays the list where all six can see it. The six then discuss that topic for four minutes. Then the other three present their topic. 4 minutes
3. The two groups of three then swap topics and lists, make new sixes and repeat step 2. 4 minutes

Activity 7 Using numbers

Topic: Numbers

Words: Numbers

Grammar: It is, it's . . ., you are . . .

Function: Saying numbers, guessing

Preparation: Copy hear-say table, rulers, measuring tape

A Telephone numbers (3 minutes)

1. Teach or revise the numbers 0 ('oh'), 1, 2, 3, 4, 5, 6, 7, 8, 9. Each student then
    writes their telephone number (or one they know) and has one minute to circulate
    and say it to five people before sitting down again. 3 minutes

Acknowledgement: David Vale

B (5 minutes)

1. Prepare a measuring tape, ruler or height chart (in centimetres) — one for each
    group of three students.
2. In their threes, the students measure each other's height in centimetres and in
    sixes they tell each other their height, e.g. 'one three five', 'one four two', 'one
    0 one'. 5 minutes

C Hear and say (5 minutes)

1. Copy the following 'hear-say' tables on to a big sheet of paper or the board.
2. The students then each make a copy of the tables.
3. Tell the students that when they *hear* a number in the left column, they must *say*
    the number in the right column. Students work in fours. They start by saying
    the top left-hand corner 'say' number 3. They can stop when they get back to
    3, or groups who finish early can try to do it again much faster. (Again make
    sure they say 'three 0 five' for 305 not 'three hundred and five'). 5 minutes

Left (Hear)	Right (Say)	Left (Hear)	Right (Say)
	3	8	5
305	425	393	4
219	444	303	505
2	999	5	767
3	305	101	202
425	219	505	404
6	404	767	393
444	2	4	101
999	6	202	303
404	576	404	787
576	8	787	3

Role-play, simulation and discussion 7

Topic:	Measuring clothes
Words:	Parts of the body, clothes
Grammar:	It is, it's, you are
Function:	Guessing, estimating measurements
Preparation:	String or measuring tapes (one per three students)

Role-play 7: The tailor (8 minutes)

1. Divide the students into groups of three (A, B and C). A is the tailor/dressmaker who measures (chest, waist, hips, leg, arm, neck). He or she says the number to B, who is the assistant, and writes them down. They they can change roles so that B is tailor, C is assistant and A is measured, then C is tailor, A is assistant and B is measured and so on. In some cultures, the groups may need to be composed of people of the same sex. 4 minutes
2. Each student then draws the clothes to be made, writing the measurements on to the drawing and the name of their customer. 2 minutes
3. Each student then shows their customer the design. 2 minutes

Simulation 7: The dress designer (6 minutes)

1. In pairs the students help each other draw stylish clothes for themselves. They write on their measurements (they may want a tight or loose fit). 3 minutes
2. In fours, each student in turn stands and models how they want the clothes to look. The other three are tailors, and look carefully at the drawing. 3 minutes

Discussion 7: Measurements (4 minutes)

Acknowledgement: David Vale

1. Ask for four volunteers to stand in front of the class. Ask one of them to say their height, then put him/her back to back with each of the other three in turn

and get the class to guess the height of each of the other three. After the guesses, the other three can say their heights. Do the same with other measurements, e.g. arm length, waist. 4 minutes

Activity 8 Teaching new items

Topic: Any, e.g. food, household objects

Words: Any, e.g. food, household objects

Grammar: Any, e.g. I am, I'm not, you are, you're not, he is, he's
                    not, I've got, I have, my, mine

Function: Describing self, indicating ownership

Preparation: Objects/pictures with cards or words on the back of the
                    pictures

A Understand, say (Action Chain) (5–10 minutes)

1. Pass the objects/pictures round, then say the words and pass the objects/pictures
   round again. Then pass the objects/pictures and say the words going in *both*
   directions. Then ask for the objects/pictures back.
2. Pass the objects/pictures round again communicating clearly the new grammar
   you want to add, e.g. hold the item to yourself and say 'I've got a . . .' or point
   to yourself and the item and say 'I am a . . .'.

B See word, read, say (Action Chain) (5–10 minutes)

1. Use picture cards with the word on the back of the picture. Pass round each word
   card and say each word. Then mix words only with word and picture, e.g. by
   flipping over the card with picture and word on opposite sides and pass them
   both ways. Ask for the objects/pictures/words back. Hold the words up, and ask
   everyone to say them.
2. Now revise any new grammar from Activity A above. You could distribute all
   but one of the items, show yours and say 'I've got a . . .' and then pass it to the
   first student. The students each say the sentence about their objects, and pass it
   around in the same direction. When your item has got back to you call 'stop!'

C Add new examples, different directions (Action Chain) (5 minutes)

1. This activity is best done immediately after Activity B above. Have ready further

objects and pictures of the same items, e.g. several cups, several combs. Distribute them among the students.

2. Step out of the chain. Show your students (many of whom have an item in their hand) that they can pass them in *different* directions and can change direction whenever they like, including passing an item back the way it came.

3. You move around slipping further items into the chain and taking out other items. In this way your students learn that the same word can refer to different examples of the same object.

Role-play, simulation and discussion 8

Topic: Any topic

Words: Any words

Grammar: Any grammar

Function: Expressing ownership

Preparation: Objects and pictures

Role-play 8: Collectors (5 minutes), Memorisers ('Kim's game') (5 minutes)

1. Use the items (objects/pictures) from Activity 8C. Give these out so each student has an equal number. The students form pairs. Each pair decides which items they want to collect. They then circulate, swapping their items until they get what they want. You model the sentences/communication you want them to use, e.g. 'Can I swap my X for your Y?'. The rule is that they must always have the same number of items they started with, i.e. they can't give any away. This familiarises the students with all the objects.
2. Put about ten of the items on a table. All students in pairs look at them for one minute. You then cover the table with a cloth/paper. The pairs draw what was where (and write the words if you wish). They can say in sentences (you model the sentences) to another pair what they think is where. You then uncover the items and everyone can look to check.

Simulation 8: Favourites (3 minutes), 'Me' (5 minutes)

1. In this simulation, the students use the items symbolically and personally so that they absorb the words and grammar into their lives, into themselves. In this way the new language items become integrated with their experience and their personalities.
2. Display all the new items. Each student silently works out their three favourites in order of preference. You model the sentences they are to use. Each student in pairs says their preferences. In new pairs each student tries to guess the other's preferences.

3. Each student works out which two, three or four items best express their personality and the pattern/design/arrangement the items would be in. They then quickly draw the pattern. You model the sentences they are to use next. In new pairs each student (a) tries to guess which the items are and is then told and (b) tries to guess the arrangement of the items and is then told.

Discussion 8: Situation and guessing (10 minutes)

1. In groups of four the students think of a situation, e.g. a desert island, a discotheque, a ship at sea, a birthday party, astronauts.
2. They then agree which of the items they would need in that situation and choose one other item not from today's lesson. You model the sentences they are to use next, e.g. 'In our situation we need X, Y and Z. Where are we?'
3. The fours make two pairs and each pair goes with another pair to make a new four. Each pair then says which items they have and the other pair tries to guess the situation. Then each pair says which other item they have. The other pair continues to try to guess the situation.
4. Each pair makes a new four with another pair but instead of just saying the items, they dramatise the situation and mention the items within their little drama.
5. The original fours then get back together to discuss their dramatisations and their success in guessing.

Activity 9 Teaching new items using pictures and objects

Topic: Any, e.g. numbers, food, household objects, clothes, shopping

Words: Any, which can be learned from a picture or object

Grammar: Any, e.g. habits, how much?, how many?, singulars, plurals

Function: Any function

Preparation: Objects and/or pictures

A   Total physical response active learning (6 minutes)

Acknowledgement: David Vale

1. Choose between five or ten new items which belong together. Objects can be toys or models, e.g. a tiny police car. Provide further examples (objects/pictures) — enough for one per student. In this first activity it is important that your students *do not* say the words. Keep them silent. They are actively learning the words.
2. Show them the items one at a time, saying the word as you show them. 20 seconds
3. Put the items one at a time where everyone can see them (e.g. on the floor around the walls) and say the word as you place each one. 20–30 seconds
4. Point to each item in turn saying the word each time. 20 seconds
5. Continue to point to each item and say each word and encourage your students to point to each item as you do. 20 seconds
6. Stop pointing but continue saying the words. Your students continue pointing. 40 seconds
7. Get your students to stand in groups near the items (e.g. on the floor or around the walls). Get each group to choose an item. Then say a word. The group with that word wave. Say the other words rapidly and get each group to wave when they hear 'their' word. 30 seconds
8. Each group moves quickly to another item. You say the word and they wave. Repeat twice. 1 minute

9. Get one group to say their own names all together. Then you say the word for their item and they say their names. You say the other words and each group says their names when they hear their word. 30 seconds

10. Each group moves quickly to another item and you say the words and they say their names. 1 minute

B   Total physical response active speaking (4 minutes)

1. Immediately after step 10 of Activity A above encourage each group to pick up their item.

2. Then encourage them to say the word quietly as they go round saying it to the other groups (who are doing the same). 30 seconds

3. Next the groups swap words with other groups as they go round and have to say the new word each time as they show and swap it. 1 minute

4. At this point while they are circulating, you give out further examples of the same items until every student has an item and is constantly swapping and saying. $2\frac{1}{2}$ minutes

C   Total physical response communicating (3 minutes)

1. After step 4 of Activity B, take one item yourself and use the new word in sentences your students know. This is the model for them to circulate, swapping and saying these sentences. 30 seconds

2. Now take one item yourself and model with clear communication a new sentence (their grammar) using the new word. Your students then communicate following your model. 2 minutes

Role-play, simulation and discussion 9

Topic: Any topic

Words: Any which can be learned from a picture or object

Grammar: Any grammar

Function: Requesting, asking, agreeing, disagreeing

Preparation: You may need props, e.g. measuring tape

Role-play 9: Using the items (5 minutes)

1. Get your students using the new items to help them gain confidence in manipulating them, e.g. if the items are numbers, they could do quick simple sums; if food or clothes, they could role-play shoppers and shopkeepers; if household objects, they could divide into pairs and one student could hide an item while the other asks questions to help him or her find it.

Simulation 9: Personalised items (10 minutes)

1. Apply the new items to a useful and personal communication about yourself and your students. For example, if you are using numbers, they could measure with measuring tapes each other's heights and stretches (finger tip to finger tip) and compare, guess and estimate. If you are using food or clothes, they could express their likes, dislikes and favourites, and discuss what is appropriate for particular occasions.

Discussion 9: Persuasion (5–10 minutes)

1. Get your students to guess, agree and disagree about their likes and dislikes. For example, one pair could persuade another pair that their opinions/guesses are correct. You could start the discussion by simply saying '... is best' and your students could then argue with you to persuade you to change your mind. Alternatively, your students could put together a situation including some of the new items and discuss the appropriateness or inappropriateness of the items.

Activity 10 I'm famous

Topic: Famous people

Words: Adjectives

Grammar: Adjectives

Function: Describing people — appearance and character interviewing

A Names and descriptions (8 minutes)

1. Brainstorm on the right-hand side of the board adjectives to describe people. 2 minutes
2. Brainstorm on the left-hand side of the board names of famous people of any nationality. 3 minutes
3. Invite the students to link any of the adjectives to the names. Draw a line between an adjective and the name that they link it with. 3 minutes

B Information gathering (4 minutes)

1. In pairs, ask the students to choose a name and prepare to say two sentences about that person. 3 minutes
2. Each student tells three other students their two sentences and then sits down again. 1 minute

C Prepare the interview (11 minutes)

1. Each student prepares between four and ten questions for an interview with a selected famous person. 3 minutes
2. Each student chooses 'to be' a famous person and prepares answers to their own questions. 3 minutes
3. In pairs (A and B), A gives B A's questions. B then asks A A's questions which A answers as if they were the famous person. They then swap roles. 5 minutes

Role-play, simulation and discussion 10

Topic: Famous people

Words: Adjectives

Grammar: It's good to be, it's bad to be, would you?

Function: Expressing advantages and disadvantages

Role-play 10: The interview (5−8 minutes)

1. After Activity 10C, the students form new pairs (A and B). A interviews B, not looking at B's questions. B answers as the famous person. They then swap. 5−8 minutes

Simulation 10: Reversed interviews (5−10 minutes)

1. The students stay in their role-play pairs. A is the famous person of their choice. A interviews B as B's self. Then B as the famous person of their choice interviews A as him or herself. 5−10 minutes

Discussion 10: Being famous (5−15 minutes)

1. In groups of six the students discuss what it is like to be famous. Would *they* like to be famous? What are the advantages and disadvantages? Is hero-worship healthy? Would they join a fan club? 5−15 minutes

Activity 11 Living spaces

Topic: House and rooms

Words: House, rooms, room contents

Grammar: That's a, this is a, these are, there's a, in/near/next to, etc

Function: Describing rooms

Preparation: On big piece of paper produce a drawing of a house including a living room, kitchen, bedroom and bathroom with labels

A Draw the room (13 minutes)

1. In pairs, the students draw one room per sheet of paper — living room, kitchen, bedroom, bathroom, and so on. In each room they draw appropriate objects and furniture with labels in English. One student from each pair can come up to look at your drawings, to ask you the names of things, and to ask how to say (pronounce) any words they are doubtful about. Everyone stops labelling and drawing after eight minutes.
2. Show your drawings one by one and point to the items. Your students point to those items in their own drawings and say the words. Some students will have items not in your drawings. They keep those secret. 5 minutes

B Share the room (9 minutes)

1. In the same pairs, the students lay out their drawings for all to see, and go round looking at the other pairs' drawings identifying the secret items. They then try to remember all the secret items they have seen after four minutes.
2. Each pair returns to their own drawings. They then add in and label all the secret items they can remember. 2 minutes
3. One pair volunteers to show their drawing and point as you did in Activity 11A while the other students say the words. Any students who still have secret items show these items and say the words themselves. 3 minutes

C Back to back dictations (9 minutes)

1. Draw a square on the board and ask what room it is. Then ask what you should draw in it. You keep asking 'where?' and giving them directions, e.g. 'You mean here in the right-hand top corner, in the middle, at the top?' 3 minutes

2. In pairs (A and B) two students sit back to back. A dictates a room in A's own house/flat which B draws. At the end of three minutes B shows the drawing to A and they discuss it. Then they swap roles. 6 minutes

Role-play, simulation and discussion 11

Topic:	House and rooms
Words:	House, rooms, contents
Grammar:	This is, that is, I want
Function:	Describing rooms and houses

Role-play 11: Interior design (14 minutes)

1. In groups of four (A B C D), A and C are interior designers and B and D are millionaires. They have two minutes to think alone in silence about ideas for rooms. Then A and C talk and draw together and B and D talk and draw together. 5 minutes
2. The four then splits into two pairs and the millionaires (B and D) tell the designers (A and C) which room they would like to be designed. They agree a drawing together. 5 minutes
3. The millionaires take each other on a guided tour of their room, while the designers show each other their drawings. 4 minutes

Simulation 11: Kidnapped! (14 minutes)

1. In new groups of four (A B C and D), all the students are themselves. A and B wake up from a drugged sleep and find they are in a small furnished house with all the doors and windows locked and barred. They do, however, have a secret radio. C and D are outside the house. C and D contact A and B on the radio. A and B explore the house, reporting what they see. C and D make notes and give advice on how to use what is in the house to be able to break out of the house. 10 minutes
2. Each group of four reports to the rest of the class on what they did to escape. 4 minutes

Discussion 11: The perfect house (13 minutes)

1. In groups of three the students agree on what they mean by 'the perfect house'. They draw it, and prepare to describe it. 8 minutes
2. In groups of nine each group of three presents their house and answers questions from the other two groups. 5 minutes

Activity 12 Islands

Topic: Escape to the island

Words: Useful objects

Grammar: Present simple, imperatives

Function: Instructing, ordering, describing actions

A Is it useful? (9 minutes)

1. Draw a picture of the country you are in, a boat and an uninhabited island. Brainstorm disasters, e.g. flood, drought, wind, fire, war, pollution, disease. 1 minute
2. Tell your students that they have each saved three things and have escaped in the boat to go to the island. They are the only people to have escaped. Put your students close together 'on the boat'. They each have to find out what three things each person has during the three minute voyage.
3. They then have a meeting on the boat to decide how the things they have brought can be used on the island. 5 minutes

B Landing on the island (13−25 minutes)

1. The students land on the island and have a meeting to decide who will do what in the first two days. 5 minutes
2. They then 'do' what is agreed (e.g. a guided fantasy) and meet again after two days and two nights on the island.
3. Each person invents one fact about the island that they have discovered. They pool information about the island and decide who will do what jobs. 8−20 minutes

C One month on (15−40 minutes)

1. Each student 'does' their agreed job for a month (e.g. a guided fantasy). The students then have a meeting where people can complain and suggest different jobs or request help. 5−10 minutes
2. The meeting then decides they need to agree ten rules (or more) for living on the island. The rules can be copied to show others. 10−30 minutes

Role-play, simulation and discussion 12

Topic: Islands

Words: Various objects and uses

Grammar: 'Will' future, 'going to' future, (must, have to)

Function: Expressing plans

Role-play 12: Explore (33–38 minutes)

1. In groups of three the students make a new plan, e.g. how to escape from the island, how to reorganise the island, how to rule the island, how to get other people there. They have ten minutes to prepare their plan. 10 minutes
2. In groups of nine each group of three presents their plan to the others. Together they agree on one of the plans to propose to the whole class. The plan may be a combination of two or three plans. 8 minutes
3. Each group of nine proposes one plan to the whole class. The whole class decides which plan to adopt. 10 minutes
4. They 'do' the plan (e.g. guided fantasy). 5–10 minutes

Simulation 12: Ten useful things (15 minutes)

1. In silence each student thinks about how they would live on a desert island, what ten things they would take there and what they would do with those things. 5 minutes
2. In groups of three each student talks for three minutes and answers questions from the others. 10 minutes

Discussion 12: Survival (10–20 minutes)

1. Discussion of 'Survival of the planet', 'New rules for society' or 'A Utopia'.

Activity 13 Information

Topic: Information desk

Words: Where? When? What? How?

Grammar: WH questions and answers

Function: Asking for and giving information

Preparation: Two copies of the information. A large diagram to stick
cards to. Question cards (two per student). Means of
sticking

A Information desk (13 minutes)

Acknowledgement: Mo Strangeman

1. At each of two separate tables a student sits at an information desk with the
information (e.g. bus/railway timetable/airport flights/tourist sights and opening
hours/map of a town/what can be bought where in a shopping complex or
department store). The other students either make their own question cards or
you give them out. While the information desk students are looking through the
information, you talk about the situation and show the class the diagram which
they will stick their card to when they have got the answer to their question (e.g.
the diagram is of the town and when they are informed where the post office is,
they stick their post office question card in the right place on the map). In larger
classes you could have pairs of students manning the information desks or increase
the number of information desks. 3 minutes
2. Each student queues up to ask their first question, then joins another queue to
ask the second question. When they have an answer, they stick their card in the
right place on the diagram. 10 minutes

B Using the information (11 minutes)

1. Give the students three minutes to look at all the cards on the diagram and to
remember all the information. 3 minutes
2. In pairs the students make up questions to ask another pair. 3 minutes

3. In groups of four each pair asks their questions of the other pair. You move around quickly arbitrating in any disputes. 5 minutes

C   What I know best (11 minutes)

1. In new pairs the students decide what they know about best (anything). They prepare to answer questions on that topic/subject and they put up a notice on their table announcing the topic e.g. stamps, cars, cats, tennis, 'my room'. 5 minutes
2. Half the pairs man their information desks. The other pairs each go to an information desk and ask questions and get answers for exactly one minute. You signal the end of the minute. All pairs move to a different information desk for one minute, then to another one for one minute. 3 minutes
3. The pairs who were giving information go round as in step 2 seeking information and the other pairs man an information desk each. 3 minutes

Role-play, simulation and discussion 13

Topic: Tourists, pen-friends

Words: Tours, tourism, then, after, before

Grammar: WH questions and answers, future

Function: Describing places, describing self, describing future plans

Role-play 13: Tourist information (17 minutes)

1. In pairs the students prepare to pretend to be tourist information officers and to answer the questions of English-speaking tourists coming to tour the area where the school is. They think up interesting tours for different types of tourist. 5 minutes
2. As in Activity 13C, half the pairs man tourist information desks. The other pairs go to one desk for two minutes, then another desk for two minutes then another for two minutes, each time asking about interesting tours in the area. 6 minutes
3. The tourists and tourist information officers swap roles and repeat step 2. 6 minutes

Simulation 13: Pen-friend's visit (9–15 minutes)

1. In groups of four (A B C and D), A and C are themselves and B and D are A and C's American/British pen-friends who know about the area but who are about to come on their first visit. A and C talk about what they will do with B and D when they come while B and D talk about what they would like to do. 3–5 minutes
2. B 'telephones' A and D 'telephones' C sitting in pairs back to back. They talk about the forthcoming visit. 3–5 minutes
3. They then swap roles and discuss together what to do during their visit. 3–5 minutes

Discussion 13: 3-week trip (15–20 minutes)

1. In new groups of four the students draw up a three week programme for a group of ten overseas students. 10 minutes
2. The fours combine into groups of eight to discuss and compare their programmes. (If possible, put the ideas into action with an exchange group.) 5–10 minutes

Activity 14 Secret objects

Topic: Objects in a bag

Words: Adjectives

Grammar: Order of adjectives

Function: Describing objects' approximations

Preparation: An opaque bag, e.g. a pillow case with ten objects in it

A   In the bag (3 minutes)

1. Put the bag where your students can see it but not the objects inside it. Begin
    a brainstorm of what might be in the bag. Rattle it and brainstorm some more
    ideas. Let some students feel the objects from the outside of the bag and brainstorm
    some more ideas. Don't say whether they are right or wrong. 3 minutes

B   Feel and describe (4 minutes)

1. Ask a student to volunteer to come up and put one hand into the bag. Ask him
    or her to feel an object and describe it. Show the object to all the students and
    put the object back in the bag. 1 minute
2. Ask another volunteer to feel another object. This time the others ask the student
    questions to elicit a description. 2 minutes
3. When they have guessed, or after between six and ten questions, show the object.
    1 minute

C   Guess and remember (6 minutes)

1. Put eight objects in the bag. In groups of three ask the students to write a list
    of what they think is in the bag. If they don't know the word in English they
    can draw it or write it in their mother tongue. 1 minute
2. Give one student from each group ten seconds to feel the objects through the outside
    of the bag. Three or four students can do this at the same time. Hold the bag
    tightly. They go back to tell their group. Now another from each group comes

up and has ten seconds to feel inside the bag. The third from each group then comes up and has five seconds to look inside the bag. They then write a second list of what they now think the eight objects are. 3 minutes

3. Now remove each object from the bag and pass it round. 2 minutes

Role-play, simulation and discussion 14

Topic: Objects in a bag

Words: Adjectives, nouns

Grammar: Why? ... because

Function: Describing what things are used for. Giving reasons

Role-play 14: Swag bag (15 minutes)

1. In pairs the students pretend they are criminals. They decide what crime they have committed, and what is in the (imaginary) bag they are carrying. They prepare to talk to the police about each thing as if they have not committed a crime. They draw each thing. 5 minutes
2. In groups of four each pair in turn pretends they are the police. They stop the other pair and demand to know what is in the bag. The 'criminals' show the drawings, and while the police question them, they try to explain innocent reasons for having the things in the bag. 10 minutes

Simulation 14: Turn out your pockets! (4−8 minutes)

1. Each student looks in their bag or pockets, or remembers what they normally keep in their bag or pockets (or what they would pack in a case for a weekend away). They prepare to talk about (and show) the contents of their bag, pockets or case. 2−4 minutes
2. In groups of three each student talks about or shows the contents of their bag, pockets or case. The others ask questions and comment on what is revealed about the person's character by the items. 2−4 minutes

Discussion 14: Classification (7−18 minutes)

1. With one person from each of the different groups of three, the students form sixes. They try to divide the class into three or four types, judging by the contents of the bags, pockets or cases. They give each type an appropriate title and prepare to report back to the class. 10 minutes

2. Each group of six reports back to the class and the class discusses their classifications. 5–8 minutes

Alternatively:

1. In groups of four, the students discuss which ten things they would pack for a particularly dangerous imaginary journey. 5–10 minutes
2. In groups of eight each four asks the others what they have packed and why. 2 minutes

Activity 15 Teaching new items using actions and movements

Topic: Any topic

Words: Any vocabulary, actions, movements, objects

Grammar: Any grammar, imperatives (initially)

Function: Instructing (initially)

A Total physical response active learning (3–5 minutes)

Acknowledgement: James Asher

1. Choose between five and seven new items which (a) belong together and (b) that you can demonstrate as actions or movements. It is important that your students remain silent.
2. Call two students as volunteers to sit or stand next to you. You do the actions and movements and they copy you. Make this a fairly predictable sequence of actions in a process. As you do each action, say the words. Do this sequence three times. Don't make any extra gestures, just the actions for the words you say. The other students just watch. They have all learned the words by now.
3. Indicate that one of the volunteers is to stay still. You now say the words staying still too.
4. The other volunteer does the actions for the words you say. Then the immobile student does the actions you say too, and the other volunteer stays still. *It is important* to create surprises and humour, so sometimes put at least one action in an inappropriate place in the sequence.
5. Lead the class in applauding the two volunteers. Now indicate that everyone must now do the actions for the words you say. The whole class does the actions twice (remember to include surprises or humour).

B Total physical response active speaking (5–8 minutes)

1. Divide the students into groups of three. In each three they take it in turn to be the 'teacher' and say the words for the other two to do the actions. While they are doing this, you go round listening and watching.

2. You become the volunteer with the class as a whole saying the words and you doing the actions. If different students are telling you to do different things at the same time, you can either wait until they agree which to say or do both actions.

C Total physical response communicating (5 minutes)

1. Your students make new groups of three. In each three they take it in turns to be the 'teacher' and say the words for the actions in different orders in the sequence. The 'teacher' says the whole sequence, then one of the other students does that sequence while the third watches to check.
2. Now add in some other words they already know so that the sequence becomes more real and useful, e.g. you say or write up these other words and they repeat step 1 integrating the new words.
3. You go round adding further new words, and saying sequences integrating the new words.

Role-play, simulation and discussion 15

Topic: Any topic, e.g. shopping

Words: Any, e.g. shopping, goods

Grammar: Any, e.g. questions, polite requests

Function: Any, e.g. buying and selling, giving advice

Role-play 15: Martians in a shop (8−12 minutes)

1. The students divide into groups of four (A, B, C and D). A and B are the earth people. C and D are Martians. A and B give C and D advice on how to cope with the situations in the role-play. For example, C has just got a job as a shop assistant. D is a customer. A instructs C and B instructs D on how to cope with the situation. 2 minutes
2. A and B then say 'Go'. If any Martian meets a situation they have not received instructions for, they come back to A or B for more instructions. 3−5 minutes
3. The two pairs swap roles and repeat the role-play. 3−5 minutes

Simulation 15: Shops (8 minutes)

1. Divide the class into two halves (A and B). The students in Group A are shop assistants. The students in group B are customers wanting to buy something they would like to buy in real life. Each customer goes into one shop and interacts with the shop assistant for a strict length of time, e.g. 90 seconds.
2. Signal the end of the time allowed. All the customers leave the first shop and go into a second (empty) shop. 90 seconds
3. Move to a new shop. 90 seconds
4. Each student pairs with a student they haven't shopped with before. Each talks, as themselves, about their experiences in the three shops.

Discussion 15: Advice on shopping (10−15 minutes)

1. In threes or fours the students discuss which specific real shops in the locality are best for what. 5 minutes
2. Each group prepares a talk (e.g. with a map) for an English tourist.
3. In sixes or eights each group reports to the other group. 5−10 minutes

Activity 16 Ecology and the environment

Topic: Pollution

Words: Chemicals, pollutants, etc

Grammar: Too much

Function: Complaining

A Pollutants: air, water, land (5 minutes)

1. Draw a circle to represent the Earth with a circle outside it to show the atmosphere. Write headings for three columns: air, water and land.
2. Mime drinking water, choking and dying. Mime breathing air, choking and dying. Mime picking a vegetable, eating it, choking and dying. Write Pollution above each column. Brainstorm pollutants or connected words for each column. Include words you know which your students don't know and communicate what the new words mean. 5 minutes

B The environmentalists speak (12 minutes)

1. In groups of three the students choose air, water or land (encourage a reasonably equal number for each heading). They then have five minutes to prepare to talk about their subject.
2. In new groups of three one student talks about air, one about water and one about land. They each talk in turn and agree one or two sentences to say to the rest of the class. 5 minutes
3. Each group says their sentences to the rest of the class. You write them down on a large piece of paper or the board. 2 minutes

C The real situation (10−15 minutes)

1. The students stay in the groups they were in for Activity 16B. Tell them they are to prepare sentences about their subject in their country. 3−5 minutes
2. All the air people make one group and share their sentences, all the water people make another group and all the land people make another group. Each group agrees on three sentences to say to the rest of the class. 5 minutes
3. Each group says their sentences. You write them down on a large piece of paper or the board. 2−5 minutes

Role-play, simulation and discussion 16

Topic:	Pollution
Words:	Chemicals, pollutants, etc
Grammar:	Present simple
Function:	Complaining, demanding, stating policies
Preparation:	Write the sentences from Activities 16B and C on a large piece of paper or the board

Role-play 16: The pressure group (15 minutes)

1. Read out the sentences. The students divide into groups of four. They are local pressure group members concerned about pollution preparing to talk to the local politicians in the village/town/city where they live. 5 minutes
2. In groups of eight, one four pretends to be the pressure group and the other four pretends to be the local politicians. They role-play in their group of eight. (They can role-play in pairs for the first two minutes if they wish). 5 minutes
3. The students form new groups of eight and each four swaps to the other role. 5 minutes

Simulation 16: One's own reaction (15–20 minutes)

1. Each student decides in two minutes' quiet what they feel about pollution and forms a sentence which expresses their view.
2. Everyone circulates, saying their sentence to everyone else. They then gather in groups with similar feelings. Each group decides on the action to be taken. 5–10 minutes
3. Each group circulates telling the other groups what they have decided to do. If real action groups emerge, let them. Be prepared for action! 8 minutes

Discussion 16: The extreme views (10 minutes)

1. Propose three or four extreme views or get one or two extrovert students to sit with you so that you can whisper the extreme views in their ears for them to say.

For example, you could pretend to be an industrialist for whom profit is the only motive and who believes others must suffer the pollution or clear it up themselves or pay you to clear it up. Or you could say that you think all industrial processes and machines should stop, all cities be closed, and everyone should return to rural self-sufficiency. 5 minutes

2. In pairs or groups of three the students have one minute to think up replies, then you argue freely with them. 5 minutes

Activity 17 Using an overhead projector

Topic: Any topic, e.g. clothes

Words: Any words, e.g. clothes, packing

Grammar: Imperatives

Function: Instructing

Preparation: (20 minutes before the lesson) Draw the items (simple outlines) on to an overhead transparency. Draw about 20 items per transparency, e.g. hat, scarf, two gloves, two socks, two shoes, shirt, sweater, trousers, jeans, handkerchief, belt, underpants, spectacles, toothbrush, towel, two boots. Colour them. Cut them out (as near the outline as you can). Have one square piece of paper about $\frac{1}{8}$ of the size of the transparency. This is the 'suitcase'.

A An untidy heap (3−5 minutes)

Acknowledgement: Ingrid Barbour

1. Put the items in an untidy heap together on the OHP. Ask your students to tell you what they can see. Each time they say the word for an item, separate it so it can be seen more clearly. At that point, name it clearly in English and talk about it in two or three sentences. 3−5 minutes

B Packing (3−5 minutes)

1. Put the suitcase on the OHP and ask which item you should put in first. Your students tell you each item to pack and you talk about it in two or three sentences as you pack it. 3−5 minutes

C Re-packing (3−5 minutes)

1. 'Oh dear!' The suitcase is packed, but you've just heard your holiday destination has been changed, e.g. beach instead of skiing, sailing instead of archaeology.

Ask your students what you should take out of the suitcase (and do so) and what new things you will need (be ready to draw them on the board). 3—5 minutes

Alternative situations are (a) a transparency figure with clothes that fit to dress for different occasions; (b) a car/bicycle in pieces that needs to be fitted together; (c) a room/house that needs to have the furniture appropriately placed; (d) a table that needs to be laid; (e) shopping for the week's food/a party; (f) shopping for Christmas (or equivalent) presents; (g) rearranging all the chairs and tables in your classroom for different activities. Some of these can be done without an OHP with a pile of objects on the floor or table.

Role-play, simulation and discussion 17

Topic: Any topic

Words: See Activity 17

Grammar: See Activity 17

Function: See Activity 17

Role-play 17: Items to pack (10−15 minutes)

1. In pairs each student folds and tears/cuts a sheet of paper into eight pieces and together they draw 16 items. You circulate giving them the words for the items to pack for a particular situation which they have chosen, e.g. a holiday. 5 minutes
2. The pairs combine into fours keeping the items and holiday destination secret. Each pair in turn asks 'Should I pack a . . .?' When the answer is 'Yes' they receive the item. The other pair can try to guess the destination at any time. The first pair to get 16 items wins. 5−10 minutes

Simulation 17: What you need (12−22 minutes)

1. Each person decides on a secret destination for a holiday and writes (or draws) 20 items they need to pack. They note (e.g. tick) which items they really have (at home) and think where they could buy, borrow or hire the other items. 5 minutes
2. In groups of three each person in turn says where they are going, which items they have already, and what else they need. If either of the other two have the items needed they can lend them to the third person. 5−12 minutes
3. As a class, give feedback on who ended up with everything they needed. Who ended up needing the most things? Can anyone else lend them? Is anyone going to the same destination as anyone else? 2−5 minutes

Discussion 17: Packing together (8−15 minutes)

1. In different groups of three the students agree on a holiday destination which they would all like to go to. They agree what they need to pack together and make a list of (or draw) the items. 5−10 minutes

2. The groups of three combine into sixes and each three talks about where they are going and what they have packed. The other three are critical and make suggestions. 3—5 minutes

Alternative situations (see also Activity 17) include (a) particular occasions to dress for; (b) what to have in/on car or bicycle, e.g. extras; (c) what furniture in what house/room; (d) what meal; (e) what party or week's meals; (f) what presents; (g) what activities in their classroom or another (class)room they all know well.

Activity 18 Using audio tapes

Topic: Any topic

Words: Any vocabulary

Grammar: Any grammar

Function: Any function

A Brainstorm (5 minutes)

1. Tell your students the title of the text on tape, and one sentence about it. Your students brainstorm what words they expect to hear. 2 minutes
2. Play the tape. Your students tell you which of the brainstormed words they did hear, and which other words they heard. 3 minutes

B Words they like (6 minutes)

1. Play the tape again after telling your students to write down the words they like. 2 minutes
2. Play the tape again so that they can write more words they like. 2 minutes
3. In pairs the students show each other the words they wrote and they say why. 2 minutes

C Making questions (12−14 minutes)

1. In pairs the students make up questions to ask another pair about the tape. 3 minutes
2. In groups of four each pair in turn asks their questions. The other pair answers as best they can. 3−5 minutes
3. Play the tape again. Let the group of four revise their questions and answers if they need to. 6 minutes

Role-play, simulation and discussion 18

Topic: Any topic

Words: See Activity 18

Grammar: See Activity 18

Function: See Activity 18

Role-play 18: In their own words (10–20 minutes)

1. Divide the students into groups so that in each group there is one student for each character on the tape. The students then choose which character they want to be and prepare to perform the story/dialogue in their own words and with a different ending. 5–10 minutes
2. Each group goes round performing for the other groups. Stop when most groups have performed the story/dialogue at least twice. 5–10 minutes

Simulation 18: What would you do? (10–20 minutes)

1. Ask 'What would *you* do?' In pairs the students decide what they would do in the same or a similar situation and prepare to perform their version. 5–10 minutes
2. When the first pair is ready, they go round performing to other pairs. Stop when most pairs have performed at least twice. 5–10 minutes

Discussion 18: Good or bad (12 minutes)

1. Take from the tape a controversial decision, e.g. 'Goldilocks walking into an empty house was bad/good'. In pairs the students prepare for a debate. Half the pairs prepare to say why it was bad, the other half prepare to say why it was good. 2 minutes
2. In groups of four, with one 'good' pair and one 'bad' pair, the students have a mini-debate. 3 minutes
3. The pairs change to make different groups of four and each pair argues the opposite point of view. 2 minutes
4. In sixes the students discuss alternative controversial decisions from the tape, e.g. 'The three bears leaving the house open was bad/good'. 5 minutes

Activity 19 Moving house

Topic: House and rooms

Words: Housework, packing

Grammar: Imperatives

Function: Instructing

A Slave driver (6 minutes)

1. Make four groups. Each group brainstorms a list of items in a different room — bedroom, bathroom, kitchen, sitting room, and so on. 3 minutes
2. You model being the slave driver as follows. You go into one of the groups and say 'What's that?' The student replies with the name of the item, and you say and mime 'Wash it/polish it/dust it!' as appropriate and keep asking different students who must all mime the action. 1 minute
3. Appoint a slave driver for each group. They follow your model. 2 minutes

B Moving house — packing (7–9 minutes)

1. Move the four groups round so they are in a different room. Appoint two students in each group as managers to manage their workers. The managers ask 'What's that?' of each worker, the worker replies, and the manager shows which (imaginary) box the item should be put in. You are overall manager and go round locking the boxes, and giving instructions to keep up the pace. 4 minutes
2. Pretend a section of the classroom is the removal truck. All the students ask appropriate questions, give instructions and mime in order to get everything packed in between three and five minutes.

C Moving in (9 minutes)

1. In pairs the students move into an empty and unfurnished house/flat. The packing cases are all around them. They talk together and mime the actions for unpacking, and arranging the furniture and items in the various rooms. 5 minutes
2. The pretend that they have one room as they want it when friends (another pair) call in to be shown round. The friends then take them to *their* house to show them their room. 4 minutes

Role-play, simulation and discussion 19

Topic: House and rooms

Words: Housework, times, money

Grammar: How long?

Function: Talking of time durations, negotiating

Role-play 19: Division of labour (10 minutes)

1. The pairs have moved into a house/flat. They both have jobs, so they make a list of the housework that needs doing, and agree who will do which. A guided relaxation is good here. You can guide the students to imagine the situation, e.g. what they can hear, see, smell, touch and taste. 4 minutes
2. The pairs make fours and tell each other what housework they have agreed to do. They discuss how many minutes per week each job takes and compare their totals. 6 minutes

Simulation 19: Hourly rates (7−8 minutes)

1. In silence, each student makes a list of who does what housework in their own house. As in the role-play, a guided relaxation is good here. 2−3 minutes
2. In pairs they say who does what, and they agree hourly rates of pay for different jobs around the house, and work out how much each person could be 'paid' for what they do in the week. 5 minutes

Discussion 19: Housework (5 minutes)

1. The pairs from the simulation make groups of four and discuss who does what housework, rates of pay and ways of reducing housework. 5 minutes

Activity 20 Good news, bad news

Topic: Good news, bad news

Words: Events

Grammar: Present perfect simple and continuous

Function: Giving information, telling news

A   TV news (12 minutes)

1. Draw a smiling face and write 'Good news' on a large piece of paper or the board. Brainstorm good news in a column, e.g. wedding, baby, cure for a disease, discovered treasure, new job, pay rise, peace. 2 minutes
2. Draw a frowning face and write 'Bad news'. Brainstorm a column of bad news, putting the bad items next to their opposites in the good column. The class adds good news to match bad news where there was no opposite. 2 minutes
3. In their pairs the students prepare a television news broadcast with about six news items. It can either be all bad, all good or a mixture of news. 4 minutes
4. In groups of six each pair performs their broadcast. 3 minutes
5. Acclaimed versions can be performed for the whole class. 1 minute

B   What do you want first? (6 minutes)

1. In new pairs each pair uses their imagination to create four items of news to tell a specific famous person. There should be two items of good news, and two of bad. (The news can be very unusual.) 4 minutes
2. The pairs combine into fours. One pair tells the other pair that they are the famous person. Then they say 'What do you want first — the good news or the bad news?' The 'famous person' answers and is told the news. Then the pairs swap roles. 2 minutes

C   The good news, the bad news (4−8 minutes)

1. Choose eight or ten volunteers who sit in a circle with you. The other students watch. Get the students in the circle to say alternately 'good news', 'bad news' once. Then give an example, such as 'The *good* news is a new baby. The *bad*

news is it has died'. In this way every other person in the circle says a piece of good news, with the person next to them saying a piece of bad news on the same subject. (You can put one or two helpers behind each person in the circle to help them think of an idea and say it.) Start the circle by saying 'The good news is I bought a new car'. The next person then has to say some bad news about the car and so on. 4–8 minutes

Role-play, simulation and discussion 20

Topic: The world

Words: Positive and negative adjectives

Grammar: Why ... because, verb 'to be' present simple

Function: Expressing opinions, beliefs, feelings

Role-play 20: A good or bad world (7 minutes)

1. In groups of four (A B C and D), A and B prepare to say ten things about why
    the world is a good place. C and D prepare to say ten things about why the world
    is a bad place. 3 minutes
2. A and C and B and D make pairs. A says a good thing and C says 'Yes but ...'
    for an appropriate bad thing to balance A's good thing, while B and D do the
    same. 2 minutes
3. B and C now make a pair. C says a good thing and B says a 'Yes but ...' bad
    thing while D and A do the same. 2 minutes

Simulation 20: Our feelings (11 minutes)

1. In silence each student prepares to say ten things they feel about the world. 3 minutes
2. In groups of three each student says what they want to say. Then the group agrees
    four or five points to say as a three, starting 'We think/feel/believe'. 5 minutes
3. In groups of nine each three says their piece. 3 minutes

Discussion 20: It's time to change the world (10–20 minutes)

1. Have either a short debate on the subject of 'the world is good/the world is bad'
    (see Activity 25) or a discussion to agree a list of six priorities of what is wrong
    with the world and the action necessary to change those wrongs. 10–20 minutes

Activity 21 Exploring choices

Topic: Choosing

Words: Any adjectives

Grammar: Present simple, comparatives

Function: Giving reasons, expressing preferences

Preparation: Clear furniture to one side if you can

A   Polarities (4 minutes)

1. The students all stand. They have to decide very quickly which side of the room
    to go to. For example, you say 'Mountains' and point to the right, and 'Sea' and
    point to the left. The students have to choose and gather on the right or left and
    talk in pairs or threes about why they chose that side. 1 minute
2. Repeat quickly, e.g. winter and summer; day and night; spring and autumn; eat
    and drink. List the choices on the board. 3 minutes

B   More choices (5−8 minutes)

1. Repeat Activity A but this time the students decide between four items with you
    pointing to the four corners or the four sides of the room e.g. blue, red, green
    and yellow; forest, beach, lake and city; north, south, east and west; morning,
    afternoon, evening and night; kitchen, sitting room, bathroom and bedroom. List
    the choices on the board. 5−8 minutes

C   Profiles (9−10 minutes)

1. In groups of four or six the students list the choices they opted for, then compare
    themselves with each other, e.g. 'I'm a mountains, winter, day, autumn, drink
    person. I'm also a blue, forest, north, evening, bathroom person'. 4 minutes
2. In new groups of three or four each student writes or thinks of a list of choices
    they guess (or remember seeing) for each of the other students in their group.
    In turn they each say their list and by question and answer compare it to the real
    list. 5−6 minutes

Role-play, simulation and discussion 21

Topic: Choosing

Words: Adjectives

Grammar: Superlatives

Function: Sloganising, persuading

Role-play 21: Slogans (16–21 minutes)

1. Choose the set of choices from Activity 21B which got most response and reaction. The students reform their groups of four and have two minutes to create a slogan encapsulating why their group is best.
2. Each group chants their slogan. Each group then has four minutes to create three other slogans which express why the other three groups are bad.
3. Each group chants their four slogans. They then have five minutes to prepare a speech or set of points to argue why their group is best and the others are bad. Each person in each group remembers the speech/points.
4. In new groups of four, each with one member from each group if possible, each student makes their speech in turn. Then the group argues freely. 5–10 minutes

Simulation 21: Individual profile (15 minutes)

1. Each student prepares a speech or points for agreement explaining why they, as an individual, are best, and all others are bad. For example, 'I'm cool. I'm calm. I move. I'm winter in the mountains. I'm autumn by the lake'. It can be a poem that describes them as a unique individual. It can be a picture with words on it. (If some students want to work with occasional help from a partner, let them.) 10 minutes
2. Either in groups of three or moving freely round the room to speak and listen, each student shares their speech or argument. 5 minutes

Discussion 21: World types (10 minutes)

1. In groups of six or eight the students try to define four or five specific types into which the whole world can be divided. They then try their theory on the other members of the class. 10 minutes

Activity 22　The weather

Topic:　　　　Weather 1

Words:　　　　Weather

Grammar:　　　Present simple, future

Function:　　　Forecasting

Preparation:　Pictures or clothes or mimes for weather. A weather map
　　　　　　　　of USA or UK

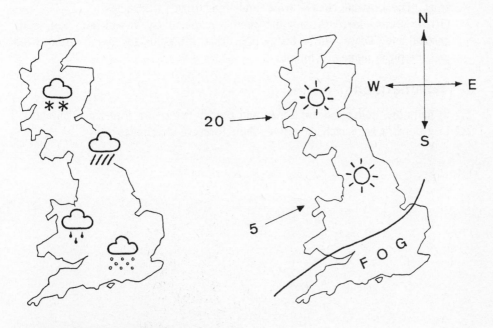

A　Weather forecast (8 minutes)

1.　Present 'rain' (e.g. using a raincoat, umbrella, picture and/or mime). Teach 'rain',
　　then say 'It's raining'. Then, as in a television weather forecast say 'It will rain
　　tomorrow'. Do the same with 'snow', 'hail', 'drizzle'. 2 minutes

2. Using the weather map the students brainstorm places, e.g. cities, areas they know. You write the words on to the map. 2 minutes
3. Give a weather forecast using the place names, e.g. in London it will rain tomorrow. In Birmingham it will drizzle. In Edinburgh it will snow. In Manchester it will hail tomorrow. 1 minute
4. Each student draws their own map of the country of their choice, writing on names of places. 2 minutes
5. In groups of three each student says a forecast. 1 minute

B   New items (6 minutes)

1. Present 'wind' (e.g. using mime, picture, overcoat, hat and scarf). Teach 'wind', then say, 'There is wind', 'Tomorrow there will be wind'. Write on the board '100 km' as a wind speed and mime or draw a tree bending. Write '200 km' and mime or draw a tree being blown over. Teach 'strong wind'. Mime or draw slates/tiles leaving a house roof (100 km) and the roof blowing off (200 km). Present 'fog', 'There is fog', 'Tomorrow there will be fog'. Demonstrate 'thick fog' and 'thin fog'. Present 'frost', 'There is frost', 'Tomorrow there will be frost'. Demonstrate 'heavy frost' and 'light frost'. 4 minutes
2. Give a weather forecast using the weather map and say 'It will rain, hail, snow, drizzle' and 'There will be heavy/light frost, thick/thin fog, wind/strong wind' and the place names. 2 minutes

C   Weathermen (5 minutes)

1. In pairs the students draw a map and prepare to give a forecast. 3 minutes
2. In groups of four each pair gives their forecast. 2 minutes

Role-play, simulation and discussion 22

Topic: Weather 1

Words: Weather

Grammar: Present simple, future

Function: Persuading, negotiating

Preparation: Six cards showing different weather

Role-play 22: **Weather gods** (10 minutes)

1. Choose six volunteers. You are chairperson. The volunteers sit around you. Give each volunteer a card. Tell them they are weather gods. The meeting is to decide the weather for tomorrow for the place your school is in. There will be different weather at different times (e.g. 6−8 a.m. frost, 8−10 a.m. snow, 10−11 a.m. fog, 11 a.m.−12 noon rain and drizzle, 12−3 p.m. wind and rain, 3−6 p.m. hail and frost, 6−10 p.m sun). Use 'There is . . .', 'It's . . .', talking about the notes you make on the timetable, and 'There will be . . .', 'It will . . .', talking from the timetable about tomorrow's weather. 5 minutes
2. In groups of seven one student is chairperson and the other six are weather gods. Each group argues to prepare *their* weather for tomorrow. The next day compare the forecast to the actual weather. 5 minutes

Simulation 22: **Weather moods** (5 minutes)

1. Write up the weather words in one column, adding any others the students know, have learned or want to know. Brainstorm and list in the next column words for emotions, feelings and moods which relate to the different weather words. You say ten sentences linking the different weather and moods, e.g. 'When it rains I feel sleepy'. 3 minutes
2. In groups of three each student talks about themselves and weather. This can lead to a class survey or questionnaire. 2 minutes

Discussion 22: Seasons (12 minutes)

1. Write 'Spring, Summer, Autumn/Fall, Winter' on the board and brainstorm appropriate jobs (1 minute), animals (1 minute), plants (1 minute), food (1 minute) and sports (1 minute). 5 minutes
2. In new groups of four the students discuss these and the weather, preparing to make statements starting 'The best weather for . . . is . . .' 'The best winter weather for . . . is . . .'. 5 minutes
3. Everyone circulates saying the sentences they have prepared. 2 minutes

Activity 23 More weather

Topic: Weather 2

Words: Speed, strength, temperature, directions

Grammar: Comparatives, superlatives

Function: Expressing numbers in words and words in numbers

Preparation: Four cards — North, South, East, West.
Four cards — hot, warm, cool, cold

A   Wind speed (7 minutes)

1. Draw a car speedometer on the board. Your students dictate where to put the numbers. 1 minute
2. Two students (A and B) volunteer. Everyone stands as trees, or puts their elbows on tables, hands in the air as trees. A varies the wind speed by pointing to the speedometer and you comment on the wind speed saying 'strong, stronger, stronger', 'gentle, more gentle'. B varies the wind direction by holding up north, south, east, west, north west etc. The students respond by moving more quickly and in different directions as appropriate. 3 minutes
3. Three students volunteer (A B and C). A and B repeat step 2. C is the wind temperature with hot, warm, cool, cold. The other students are themselves, e.g. sitting on the beach or walking in the woods. They react to wind speed, direction and temperature. 3 minutes

B   Thermometer (6 minutes)

1. Draw a big thermometer on the board. Your students dictate where to put the numbers (degrees). Take the cards hot, warm, cool and cold. Your students tell you where (which numbers) to put against the thermometer for each temperature. 2 minutes
2. A volunteer points to the temperature. The other students are themselves, e.g. waiting in a bus queue or lying in a bath. They react to temperature. 2 minutes
3. You do the same as the volunteer, but you say (dramatically) 'Hot, hotter, hotter,

cool, cooler, cooler, cold, colder, colder, warm, warmer, warmer, hot, hotter, hotter,' and so on as you point. 2 minutes

C   Temperature and wind speed (8 minutes)

1. In pairs the students decide on an exact wind speed, direction and temperature. They then change to another set of figures. They prepare to mime the first state, the change and the second state. 3 minutes

2. In groups of six each pair in turn does their mime. The other two pairs try to guess the two wind speeds, the two wind directions and the two temperatures. The miming pair are allowed to say 'Hotter, warmer, colder, cooler, stronger, more gentle', and so on until the right figures are guessed. 5 minutes

Role-play, simulation and discussion 23

Topic: Weather 2

Words: Sports, weather

Grammar: Comparatives, superlatives

Function: Complaining

Role-play 23: Just the weather for sailing! (10 minutes)

1. The students divide into groups of three. One group volunteers to be the 'weather controllers'. The other groups choose for themselves an outdoor activity, e.g. playing tennis, skiing, lying on the beach, having a barbecue, sailing. Each group decides the ideal temperature, wind speed and direction, and the percentage of humidity for their activity. Meanwhile, the weather controllers draw a humidity scale and show figures of wind speed, direction, temperature and humidity and get ready to change these regularly. 2 minutes
2. The weather controllers change the figures and the groups can go up and complain: 'We are trying to', 'We can't . . . when the . . .' and request: 'Please change the . . . to . . . . We want it cooler and drier'. The weather controllers keep changing the figures and talking, trying to please everyone. 8 minutes

Simulation 23: Internal weather (8 minutes)

1. You say what you are like, e.g. 'In the morning I'm like fog. Then I'm a 3 km wind for coffee. Then I'm 100 km wind to get ready for school. At school I'm a damp hot 50 km wind. At lunch I'm a fog with rain. In the afternoon . . .' and so on, meanwhile drawing a weather graph, e.g. a wind speed line on a graph, with symbols for rain and figures, degrees C for temperature. 2 minutes
2. In groups of three each student draws their day's graph of internal weather. You go round with further suggestions, e.g. a sun symbol as a smile received, a frost symbol for someone being unfriendly. 4 minutes
3. Each student shows their graph to the others and talks about it.

Discussion 23: Pyramid discussion (23 minutes)

1. The topic is 'How to have a perfect day no matter what the weather'. In groups of five or six the students discuss and draw up ten rules for coping with the weather, e.g. if it rains, smile, if it snows, play. 10 minutes
2. The groups combine into tens or twelves to agree ten rules together. 5 minutes
3. These groups then combine again to agree ten rules together. 5 minutes
4. The ten rules finally agreed upon are displayed. They can be copied and circulated round the school, and quoted from each day depending on the weather. 3 minutes

Activity 24 Songs, poems, texts 1

Topic: Any song/poem/text

Words: Any vocabulary

Grammar: Any grammar

Function: Meaning in intonation

A Clap the rhythm (5–11 minutes)

1. Take a particular phrase or sentence from the song/poem/text and clap out the rhythm. Get your students to copy the rhythm. Each time you give the model for them to clap, substitute one more of the words (e.g. clap clap clap clap clap clap, to clap clap clap clap clap, to be clap clap clap clap, to be or clap clap clap, to be or not clap clap, to be or not to clap, to be or not to be). They copy you each time. Take two more phrases or sentences and do the same. 3 minutes
2. Play or read aloud the song/poem/text twice. The first time the students just listen. The second time they say the phrases/sentences they have been practising. 2–8 minutes

B Intonation (5–11 minutes)

1. With lines drawn on the board, or with your hand in the air, trace the intonation pattern of another phrase or sentence. Say la la la la la in the intonation pattern. Get your students to copy the intonation, then progressively substitute the words (e.g. la la la la la, that la la la la, that is la la la, that is the la la, that is the question). Your students copy you each time. Take two more phrases or sentences and do the same. 3 minutes
2. Play or read aloud the whole song/poem/text. The first time your students listen. The second time they say all the phrases/sentences they have been practising for rhythm and intonation. 2–8 minutes

C Clap the poem (9–21 minutes)

1. You will need to practise step 2 before you do it in class.
2. Using the rhymes, or particularly key words, in the song/poem/text, recite the

whole thing *as claps* except for all those rhymes or key words you have chosen. Say these aloud quite slowly at the point at which they occur among the claps. The second time do the same, but ask your students to join in saying those words. 2−8 minutes

3. Repeat step 2 but use 'la' in the intonation pattern. 2−8 minutes
4. Ask your students to recite/sing the whole song/poem/text together twice. 5 minutes

Role-play, simulation and discussion 24

Topic: Any song/poem/text

Words: Any vocabulary

Grammar: Any grammar

Function: Expressing opinions, responding to experience

Role-play 24: Slogans (9 minutes)

1. In groups of three or four the students choose one part of the song/poem/text. They have three minutes to prepare a slogan to chant to persuade the others that their part is best. Each group chants their slogan in turn twice. 4 minutes
2. Each group is given five minutes to prepare several phrases or sentences as a short speech to say why their part is best. Each group makes their speech in turn. 5 minutes

Simulation 24: Personal response (18–35 minutes)

1. Each student selects a partner. Each student works to create their own response to the whole song/poem/text but can refer to their partner for help or work more closely with them. 10–20 minutes
2. In groups of four each student shares their responses. 8–15 minutes

Discussion 24: Shared response (5–15 minutes)

1. In new groups of three the students discuss the song/poem/text and the responses to it they have had. 5–15 minutes

Activity 25 Instant debate

Topic: Debates

Words: Any vocabulary

Grammar: Any grammar

Function: Arguing, persuading, rhetoric

A 30 second debate (2 minutes)

1. This is instant training for debates. Ask five students (A, B, C, D and E) to face the class. Using words they know, give a debate topic by whispering the words to the five students, e.g. A: 'Debate. School is good. (B's name)', B: 'School is good', A: '(C's name)', C: 'School is bad'. A: '(D's name)', D: 'School is very good', A: '(E's name)', E: 'School is very bad'. A: 'Vote, School is good? Yes?' (counts hands), 'School is bad? No?' (counts hands). A: 'Debate school is good' (or school is bad if the class so votes). 1 minute

2. In groups of five the other students follow this model. 1 minute

B Another 30 second debate (3 minutes)

1. Repeat with another topic. 3 minutes

C 3 minute debate (6 minutes)

1. Repeat as Activity 25A but add more of the formalities of debating, whispering two or three words at a time, e.g. A: 'Hello, ladies and gentlemen. The debate today is "War is good". I ask (B's name) to propose'. B: 'Mister/madam Chairman, ladies and gentlemen. I propose "War is good". War is good because war reduces population'. A: 'Thank you (B's name). I ask (C's name) to oppose'. C: 'Mister/madam Chairman, ladies and gentlemen. I oppose "War is good". War is bad because it destroys the environment'. A: 'Thank you (C's name). I ask (D's name) to second'. D: 'Mister/madam Chairman, ladies and gentlemen. I propose "War is good". War is good because it advances technology'. A: 'Thank you (D's name). I ask (E's name) to second'. E: 'Mister/madam Chairman, ladies and gentlemen. War is bad because it kills families'. A: 'Does anyone want to

speak?' (Teacher goes to whisper behind students F, G and H in the class.) F: 'Mister/madam Chairman. (E's name) says war kills families. War is bad. So war reduces population. War is good'. G: 'Mister/madam Chairman. War helps industry'. H: 'Mister/madam Chairman. Make love not war'. A: 'Vote. War is good? Yes? (counts hands) War is bad? (counts hands). War is bad . . . votes to . . .' (or war is good if the class so votes). 3 minutes

2. Repeat step 1 with pauses to encourage students A, B, C, D and E and the other students to remember what to say, and to add more reasons of their own to the reasons you whisper. Be very strict that students B, C, D and E must say *only* what fits the side they are on. It is in your strictness that they learn that *debate* is an adversarial points-scoring battle of speech skills, not a discussion of real opinions. 3 minutes

Role-play, simulation and discussion 25

Topic: Debates

Words: Any vocabulary

Grammar: Any grammar

Function: Persuading

Role-play 25: 5 minute debate (10 minutes)

1. The students divide into groups of five: Chairman, proposer and second, opposer and second. Each group prepares the same topic. (Have some topics ready, e.g. school is good, war is good, pop music is good, football is good.) While the proposers and seconds are preparing what to say, you gather all the chairmen together and teach them to say: 'The motion is . . . I ask . . . to propose the motion . . . I ask . . . to oppose the motion . . . I open the debate to the house'. 5 minutes
2. One group volunteers or is 'volunteered' to run the debate. The other students have the chance to speak when the chairman opens the debate to the floor. Be very strict with time by sitting behind the chairman and whispering in his/her ear.

Simulation 25: Preparation (20−40 minutes)

1. In groups of five the students choose a subject and prepare a five minute debate. 10 minutes
2. Each group runs a five minute debate, e.g. five minutes in each of the next six lessons. 10−30 minutes

If the debates are spread over the next six lessons, you can let them go longer each time, e.g. 5 minutes, 6 minutes, 7 minutes, 8 minutes, 9 minutes, 10 minutes.

Discussion 25: Not a debate (5−20 minutes)

1. A discussion is quite different from a debate. After a debate has been voted on, gather in a circle and start a discussion about what everyone thinks. The aim is to share their experiences rather than to try to score points. 5−20 minutes

Activity 26 Pollution

Topic: Pollution and work

Words: Any vocabulary

Grammar: Second conditional

Function: Reasoning, speculating

A Against the odds (8 minutes)

1. Ask your students 'In Mexico City the birds fall out of the air dead. Why?'. When they have answered, say 'The people continue to live in Mexico City. Why?'. When they have answered, say 'They trained chimpanzees to work in a factory. The chimpanzees stopped after one week. Why?'. When they have answered (the chimps were bored), say 'Men and women work in the factory. They don't stop. Why?'. 2 minutes
2. In pairs the students say to each other 'If I was/were a bird I would . . .' (you can model some examples). Then they say 'If I was/were a chimpanzee I wouldn't . . .'. 1 minute
3. Combine the pairs into fours and encourage lots of other ideas for 'If I was/were a chimpanzee I wouldn't . . .', e.g. go to school, wear clothes, sleep in a bed, got to the cinema. The class listens to the most interesting ones from the fours. 5 minutes

B The frogs (9 minutes)

B The frogs (9 minutes)

1. Tell this story (copy or show the drawing to help). 'There were two frogs. One was in a pan of cold water. The cold water was on the stove and the water very slowly got hotter and hotter. The frog didn't jump out. The frog died. They dropped the other frog into hot water. It jumped out immediately'. 1 minute
2. In groups of three the students make up a similar story about two people, one who never escaped, and one who did. Encourage the groups to do their own brainstorm, then to prepare a story to tell. 5 minutes
3. Each group goes round telling at least two other groups their story. 3 minutes

C Dialogues (11 minutes)

1. The pairs from Activities 26A and 26B write the beginning (e.g. eight lines) of a dialogue between either a chimp and a human, two chimps, a chimp and one of the frogs, the two frogs, a frog and a human, or two humans. 5 minutes
2. In fours each pair gives the other pair their dialogue. In turn each pair performs the dialogue and continues the situation beyond what is written. 4 minutes
3. The class can all watch repeat performances of the acclaimed best dialogues. 2 minutes

Role-play, simulation and discussion 26

Topic: Robots, animals and the future

Words: Any vocabulary

Grammar: Future, should, shouldn't, can, can't

Function: Describing

Role-play 26: Division of labour in the future (9 minutes)

1. In groups of three the students choose who is a robot, who is a human, and who is the director of the play/dialogue. They prepare, but do not write down, dialogue and interaction between the human and the robot. 5 minutes
2. Each group goes round performing to at least three other groups. 4 minutes

Simulation 26: The future (7 minutes)

1. Each student imagines him or herself ten years into the future. In silence each thinks of what their life and work might be like. 2 minutes
2. In groups of three the students ask and answer questions about the imagined futures. 5 minutes

Discussion 26: Dividing labour (11−18 minutes)

1. In new groups of four the students draw diagrams depicting their ideas on:
   - What should robots do in the future?
   - What should humans do in the future?
   - What should animals do in the future?

   8 minutes
2. In groups of eight they show and discuss their ideas. 3−10 minutes

Activity 27 Favourites

Topic: Favourites

Words: Colours, animals, English songs

Grammar: Comparatives, superlatives

Function: Comparing, expressing preferences

Preparation: Think of and note your first three favourite colours, animals and English songs

A Favourites (11 minutes)

1. Draw a grid divided into nine boxes. Along the top, outside the grid, write 'colour', 'animal', 'English song'. Down the left-hand side write 'first favourite', 'second favourite', 'third favourite'. Your students each copy the grid, large enough to write in. 1 minute
2. You write your favourites in order e.g.

	colour	animal	English song
1st favourite	green	horse	Yesterday
2nd favourite	blue	cat	The Wall
3rd favourite	red	dog	Greensleeves

and talk about why you like them. 2 minutes
3. Each student fills in their grid while you circulate, helping them with vocabulary. 3 minutes
4. When the first student is ready, they go round showing their grid and talking to others until almost everybody has shown and talked to at least two other people. 5 minutes

B   Self-image (12 minutes)

1.   Divide the students into fours. Write down the right-hand side of your grid 'How you want others to see you'. Interpret your own three first favourites as the self-image that you want to project to the world. In their fours the students share their first favourites and talk about them. 4 minutes
2.   Write 'How others see you' and interpret your three second favourites as how others view and perceive you. The students share these as before. 4 minutes
3.   Write 'How you really are' and interpret your third favourites as your real self. Your students share these as before. 4 minutes

   Don't be too serious about all this — laughter is appropriate.

C   How others see us (7 minutes)

1.   In silence each student thinks about their self-image, how they are perceived by others and how they really are. They prepare to talk. 3 minutes
2.   In groups of three each student talks about him or herself. 4 minutes

Role-play, simulation and discussion 27

Topic: Self-image

Words: Any vocabulary

Grammar: Modals would, could, can

Function: Constructing possible realities

Role-play 27: Self-representation (10−18 minutes)

1. In the same groups of three, the students prepare a trialogue or trialogues. They can either play the three aspects of one student and do it at some length, or they can play the three aspects of each of the three students more briefly. 5−10 minutes
2. In groups of nine each three performs their trialogue(s). The other two threes try to guess who is the real person each time. 5−8 minutes

Simulation 27: An ideal self (6 minutes)

1. In silence each student thinks of how or who they want to be and how and who they are. (They can draw to help their thinking.) They prepare to talk about or role-play this. 2 minutes
2. In groups of three each student role-plays or talks about him or herself. 4 minutes

Discussion 27: Guarding the self (5−15 minutes)

1. Discuss either 'You can't be famous *and* real' or 'The private lives of famous people should be private/public' or 'How to be yourself'. Discuss as a whole class or in fives, reporting to the whole class on the same or different topics. 5−15 minutes

Activity 28 Differences and stereotypes

Topic: Men and women/boys and girls

Words: Characteristics

Grammar: Present simple, comparatives

Function: Clichés

A Stereotypes (5 minutes)

1. In groups of five the students brainstorm the stereotyped differences between men and women (or for younger students, boys and girls). They make two lists, one the stereotypical characteristics of men, the other the stereotypical characteristics of women. 4 minutes
2. Each group sends out spies to collect items from the other groups' lists. 1 minute

B Vive la différence! (4 minutes)

1. The students divide into two groups. One group argues for two minutes that women are best. The other group argues for two minutes that men are best.
2. The two groups swap arguments. 2 minutes

C Stock responses (4 minutes)

1. Everybody stands in one big circle. You announce that when anyone thinks of what women stereotypically say to men, they take one step forward and say it. Everyone then steps forward, imitates them and steps back. You give an example, e.g. 'Park the car!'. 2 minutes
2. Next, look at what men stereotypically say to women. You model, e.g. 'Where are my socks?'. 2 minutes

Role-play, simulation and discussion 28

Topic: Men and women/boys and girls

Words: Any vocabulary

Grammar: Any grammar

Function: Expressing wishes, complaining, problem-solving

Role-play 28: An argument (9 minutes)

1. In groups of three one student plays a woman, one plays a man, the other gives ideas. The man and the woman talk and argue (e.g. about who is best, who will use the car or which television programme to watch). 3 minutes
2. They then swap roles and change the topic. Role-play. 3 minutes
3. One last change of role so that everyone has played all roles. 3 minutes

Simulation 28: Agony aunt (8–10 minutes)

1. In pairs the students prepare a real 'agony aunt' problem which one of them has about men or women (or boys and girls). They prepare to 'phone in'! 5 minutes
2. In groups of four one pair phones the other pair. The second pair acts as the agony aunt. Then they swap roles. 3–5 minutes

Discussion 28: Harmony or compromise? (10–20 minutes)

1. In new groups of six the students try to produce solutions for some of the problems between men and women (or boys and girls). 5 minutes
2. Each six reports their solutions to the rest of the class. 5–15 minutes

Activity 29 USA and UK

Topic: USA and UK

Words: Places, objects

Grammar: Any grammar

Function: Any function

Preparation: An outline map of USA and of UK.
                  An American song and a British song

A Maps (8 minutes)

1. Draw or put up the outline maps of USA and UK. Half the class gather round one map and half round the other map. Each group appoints two scribes who write on the map the places their group knows. 3 minutes
2. The groups and scribes then work on the other map. 2 minutes
3. The groups and scribes sit down. You read out (and correct) what they have written, and elicit some more information which you write up on the maps. 3 minutes

B Typical things (6 minutes)

1. In groups of four the students have to think of American (USA) things and say them in their groups, e.g. movies, movie stars, songs, singers, television programmes, television stars, cartoon characters. 3 minutes
2. In new groups of four they think about British things and say them. 3 minutes

C Songs (8 minutes)

1. Prepare an American and a British song.
2. Sing together an American song and a British song they all know. 8 minutes

Role play, simulation and discussion 29

Topic:	USA and UK
Words:	Any vocabulary
Grammar:	Comparatives, present simple
Function:	Arguing, comparing

Role-play 29: Extreme views (11 minutes)

1. In groups of four (A, B, C and D) A and B have to think of ten reasons why America and Americans are best, while C and D have to think of ten reasons why Britain and British people are best. 3 minutes
2. A, B, C and D then argue. 3 minutes
3. Have a minute's silence in which the students 'become' an American or a British person.
4. Make new American or British fours and argue again, this time *as* Americans and British people. 4 minutes

Simulation 29: Likes and dislikes (7—9 minutes)

1. Each student thinks for one minute about what they like about USA and UK, then for one minute about what they dislike about USA and UK, then for one minute about whether they would like to be American or British. They can take notes. 4 minutes
2. In groups of three the students talk about their ideas. 3—5 minutes

Discussion 29 (15—20 minutes)

1. Have a debate on either 'USA is better than UK' or 'The USA with 10% of the world's population uses 40% of the world's resources. Why?' or 'Our country should be like the USA'. 15—20 minutes

Activity 30 Using newspapers/magazines 1

Topic: Newspapers 1

Words: Any vocabulary

Grammar: Any grammar

Function: Expressing understanding

Preparation: An authentic newspaper or magazine article — a different one for every two students

A Words you know (6 minutes)

1. In pairs, tell your students *not* to read the article. Give them the article. Ask them to go through it underlining words they recognise (i.e. international words, cognates, words they know). 2 minutes
2. Stop everyone when the first pair has finished. Ask them to count all the words they have underlined, e.g. ten. Then ask them to count all the words they have looked at so far, e.g. 100. Then put the first number over the second, e.g. 10/100 and make a percentage, e.g. $10/100 \times 100 = 10\%$. Say 'Good, you already know 10% of the words'. 2 minutes
3. In groups of four the students look at the underlined words and the pairs tell each other what the article is about. 2 minutes

B Guessing the content (5 minutes)

1. After Activity 30A, the pairs go through the article again, underlining words which look similar to words they know in their own language or for which they can correctly guess the meanings. 1 minute
2. As in Activity 30A, do a count and percentage. You say 'Good. When you look closely, you know 20% of the words'. 2 minutes
3. The pairs combine to make groups of four and, just using the words they have underlined, they tell each other what the story is about. 2 minutes

C **Percentage understanding** (10 minutes)

1. The pairs read carefully through the whole article. Don't help them. Ask them to underline any other words for which they can guess the meaning. They then read the whole article quickly again for the whole sense. 4 minutes
2. Each pair goes to a new pair to make a four and they tell each other what the story is about. 4 minutes
3. They count up all the words they have underlined and express them as a percentage. You say 'Without help you understand 40% of the words and 60% of the story. Well done!'. 2 minutes

Role-play, simulation and discussion 30

Topic: Newspapers 1

Words: Any vocabulary

Grammar: Any grammar

Function: Telling news

Role-play 30: Reading in a café (5—8 minutes)

1. After Activities 30A, 30B and 30C the students make new groups of three. Each student has heard three stories and knows their own story. They are three friends in a café, each reading (pretending to read) a newspaper. They look up now and then and tell one another the stories they know. (Some will know the same stories as each other.) (They can start with 'It says here . . .' or 'Have you heard about . . .?'). 5—8 minutes

Simulation 30: News items (9 minutes)

1. Each person thinks of international, national, local or personal news from the last week or so, and prepares to talk about it in their mother tongue. 1 minute
2. Each student talks about the news item in a group of three. 3 minutes
3. In new groups of three, the student talks about the same news item, but this time in English. 3 minutes
4. In new groups of three, each student talks again in English. 2 minutes

Discussion 30: News broadcast (10 minutes)

1. In new groups of four the students put together a one minute radio or television news broadcast followed by radio or television discussion/interviews on the news stories. 5 minutes
2. In groups of twelve each four performs their news and discussion. 5 minutes

Activity 31 Using newspapers/ magazines 2

Topic: Newspapers 2

Words: Any vocabulary

Grammar: Any grammar

Function: Telling news

Preparation: An authentic newspaper or magazine article — a different one for each student

A Accumulating words (4 minutes)

1. Give out the articles face down. Each student has pen and paper ready. They have to look for the words they recognise and to write them down with space in order on the paper. 1 minute
2. They pass the article and paper to the next student who looks first at the paper, then at the article, and has to add more words to the list *in order*. 2 minutes
3. They pass the article and paper to the next student who looks first at the paper, then at the article; and has to add more words to the list in order starting from the end of the article and reading backwards. 1 minute

B Write your own article (12 minutes)

1. After Activity 31A, each student passes on the paper list only. They read the words on the new list, and write sentences (on the paper) made from those words. 3 minutes
2. Each student then passes the *article only* to the student who has just made the sentences. Each person compares their sentences to the article. 3 minutes
3. Each student passes the sentences and the article to the next student who reads the article first, then the words and sentences on the paper. 3 minutes
4. Each student finds a partner and tells them what the article says. 3 minutes

C Their own stories (15 minutes)

1. Put away the articles and the pieces of paper from Activities 31A and 31B. Each student makes up a story. 2 minutes

2.   Each student writes a list of words in order from their story on to a piece of paper.
     2 minutes
3.   They pass the list to the next student who thinks what the story could be about,
     and writes sentences on the paper using the words on the list. 3 minutes
4.   They pass the paper back to the original student. Each student reads the sentences,
     and writes more sentences that are either from their original story, or new sentences
     in the new story. 3 minutes
5.   Each student finds a partner and shares the list of words, then tells the original
     story or the new story. Their partner has to guess if it is the original story or
     the new story. 5 minutes

Role-play, simulation and discussion 31

Topic:	Newspapers 2
Words:	Any vocabulary
Grammar:	Any grammar
Function:	Telling news
Preparation:	Any pictures, e.g. cut from magazines or newspapers, at least one per student

Role-play 31: News pictures (9 minutes)

1. Lay out the pictures. Each student chooses a picture and makes a pair with a student with a similar or related picture. 1 minute
2. Each pair makes up a newspaper-style story to go with the two pictures. 5 minutes
3. When the first pair is ready, they go around the other pairs showing their pictures and telling their stories. 3 minutes

Simulation 31: It happened to me! (8 minutes)

1. Each student thinks of a real or imagined story about themselves, and draws a picture to represent the newspaper photograph that goes with that story. 3 minutes
2. In groups of three each student shows their picture and tells their story. The other two try to guess if the story is real or imagined. 5 minutes

Discussion 31 (10–15 minutes)

1. Discuss either 'Is what is in newspapers true?' or 'How we can make our own student newspaper?'. Or have a debate on 'Newspapers are bad'.

Activity 32 Your problems solved

Topic:　　　　　Problem-solving

Words:　　　　　Any vocabulary

Grammar:　　　　Should, could

Function:　　　　Giving advice

Preparation:　　Think of a problem you have

A Problem shared (13—18 minutes)

1. Talk about your problem (e.g. whether to sell your car and buy another, what to buy a friend as a present, what to wear to a particular event, where to go on holiday). 3 minutes
2. Ask your students to talk about your problem in groups of three and to give you advice and help. Go round during this only answering questions. 3 minutes
3. The threes combine to make sixes and they agree on the advice to give. 2 minutes
4. The groups of six report to you, and you discuss their advice. 5—10 minutes

B Giving advice (3—6 minutes)

1. In the groups of six each student thinks in silence of a problem they have. 1 minute
2. One or two students in each group of six talk about their problem and the others advise them. 2—5 minutes

C Comparing advice (5—8 minutes)

1. The students who talked about their problems in Activity 32B swap places with 'problem sharers' from another group. Each group asks questions to try to find out what the problem was, and what advice was given. 5—8 minutes

Role-play, simulation and discussion 32

Topic: Problem-solving

Words: Any vocabulary

Grammar: Should, could

Function: Asking for and giving advice

Preparation: Examples of problem pages from magazines

Role-play 32: Solving your problems (3–5 minutes)

1. In pairs the students prepare a problem that parents have with childen, children with parents, pupils with teachers, teachers with pupils. They prepare a short dialogue that shows the problem. 3–5 minutes

Simulation 32: Acting out the problem (8–10 minutes)

1. In new pairs the students prepare a problem which one of them has with another person. They prepare a short dialogue which shows the problem. 5 minutes
2. In groups of four each pair performs the problem. The others give advice. 3–5 minutes

Discussion 32: Problem pages (13–15 minutes)

1. Show some examples of problem pages from magazines.
2. In groups of six each person writes a problem page letter to an agony aunt. 3–5 minutes
3. In groups of six the students discuss and decide on appropriate replies for each letter in turn. 10 minutes

Activity 33 Mixed language stories

Topic: Mixed language stories

Words: Any vocabulary

Grammar: Any grammar

Function: Story-telling

Preparation: Prepare a story you want to tell with two or more pictures
                    or drawings. Practise telling it as in Activities 33A and
                    33B

A   Story without end (2−5 minutes)

1. Tell the story in the students' mother tongue *except* replace mother tongue words
    with those English words your students already know. Say any words in English
    which the pictures/drawings show. Omit the ending of the story. 2−5 minutes

B   More English words (4−10 minutes)

1. Tell the story again as in Activity 33A but substitute between five and ten key
    words with English words. 2−5 minutes
2. Tell the story again but substitute ten to fifteen more words with English words.
    2−5 minutes

C   All the story in English (7−16 minutes)

1. Tell the story again in English and include the ending. 2−5 minutes
2. Tell the story again in English, pausing every five words or so for your students
    to say the word that is coming next before you say it. Omit the ending. 2−5 minutes
3. In groups of three one student volunteers to tell the story and the ending in English.
    3−6 minutes

Role-play, simulation and discussion 33

Topic:	Mixed language stories
Words:	Any vocabulary
Grammar:	Any grammar
Function:	Story-telling

Role-play 33: Mixed language stories (14–18 minutes)

1. In pairs the students prepare to tell a story using mixed languages. They use the English words they already know and draw pictures of key words. To learn the key words in English they ask you or look them up in a dictionary. They prepare to tell the story three times — the first time completely in their mother tongue without the pictures and without the ending; the second time in mixed languages with the pictures and without the ending; the third time in mixed languages with the ending (and the ending if possible all in English). 10 minutes
2. The pairs get together to make fours and tell their story three times as prepared. 4–8 minutes

Simulation 33: Their own stories (15–18 minutes)

1. In pairs each student prepares their own story with the help of their partner. The story is something they would want to say about themselves to an English-speaking person who had become their friend. With the help of their partner, they prepare to communicate it as best they can, using all the English they know, drawings, mime, noises and referring to a dictionary (i.e. it can have mother tongue words in it, but their meaning must be communicated in the telling). 10 minutes
2. In groups of four each pair tells their story to the other pair. During the story, or afterwards, the listeners can ask (as if they only understood English) 'What does . . . mean?'. 5–8 minutes

Discussion 33: Coping (13–18 minutes)

1. This is in the students' mother tongue. In threes, the students make a list of all

the situations they think they *could* cope with if they arrived in an English-speaking country the next day. 3 minutes

2. In sixes they share their lists, and make a list of what they feel they *couldn't* cope with. 5 minutes
3. In twelves they look at some of the situations they think they couldn't cope with and work out how they *could* cope with them. 5–10 minutes

Activity 34 Story without its end

Topic: Story-telling

Words: Any vocabulary

Grammar: Any grammar

Function: Any function

Preparation: Prepare a story to tell

A Mixed language story (3–5 minutes)

1. Tell a story (using mixed languages if you like — see Activity 33). Omit the ending.
    3–5 minutes

B Their response (5–7 minutes)

1. Each student has pen and paper. You tell the story again omitting the ending and
    each student writes down in words, or draws, their response to the story. 3–5
    minutes
2. In groups of three each student talks about or shows their response to the story.
    2 minutes

C Story recall (18–22 minutes)

1. Tell the story again omitting the ending, and pausing for ten to twenty seconds
    after each paragraph (or similar sized section) for the groups of three to silently
    recall and remember it. 4–6 minutes
2. In groups of three the students re-tell the story and create an ending. 5 minutes
3. Each group of three goes to two other groups to tell the story with the ending
    they have created. 8–10 minutes
4. You tell the ending. 1 minute

Role-play, simulation and discussion 34

Topic: Story-telling

Words: Any vocabulary

Grammar: Any grammar

Function: Any function

Role-play 34: Story with a difference (10 minutes)

1. In new groups of three the students prepare to perform the story but they must change at least three things in it. 5 minutes
2. Each group of three performs their new version of the story for two other groups. 5 minutes

Simulation 34: How I felt (7–10 minutes)

1. Each student either imagines the story happened to them or thinks of a similar story which did happen to them. 2 minutes
2. In groups of three each student tells their story and how they felt. They ask each other questions. 5–8 minutes

Discussion 34: Conch shell (10 minutes)

1. In new groups of six each group has an object (the conch shell from *Lord of the Flies*). Only the person holding the conch shell can speak. Each speaker has to reach for it and hold it while he or she speaks. The groups discuss freely the story, the possible endings, their own stories and feelings. 10 minutes

Activity 35 Story—information gap

Topic: Story-telling

Words: Any vocabulary

Grammar: Any grammar

Function: Any function

A Telling a story (5 minutes)

1. Tell a one minute story very quietly using plenty of adjectives. While you tell it, half the students close their eyes and block their ears. 1 minute
2. The students who heard (hearers) make pairs with the non-hearers and re-tell the story (they have 30 seconds to prepare it) changing at least three things in the story. 2 minutes
3. The non-hearers partner a new hearer and re-tell the story as well as they can remember it. 1 minute
4. You re-tell the story to all the students. 1 minute

B Re-telling stories (8 minutes)

1. Prepare four different one minute stories so that each student has one story.
2. Give each student a one minute story to tell (or they can think up their own).
3. In groups of four (A, B, C and D), A tells B their story while C tells D their story. 1 minute
4. B tells C A's story (as well as he or she can remember) and D tells A C's story. 1 minute
5. C tells A A's story and A tells C C's story. 1 minute

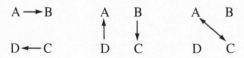

6. A then tells A's story to all and shares how much A's story has changed, and C tells C's story to all and shares how much C's story has changed. 4 minutes

C **Further re-telling** (8–10 minutes)

1. After Activity 35B, students B and D tell their stories but add a further stage.
2. B tells C B's story, C tells D B's story, D tells A B's story, A tells B B's story. Meanwhile D tells A D's story, A tells B D's story, B tells C D's story, C tells D D's story. 4 minutes

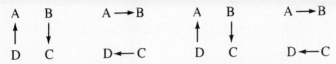

3. B re-tells B's story and comments on the changes. D re-tells D's story and comments on the changes. 4–6 minutes

Role-play, simulation and discussion 35

Topic: Story-telling

Words: Any vocabulary

Grammar: Any grammar

Function: Any function

Role-play 35: More stories with a difference (11–13 minutes)

1. In groups of four (A B C and D), A and B prepare together a one minute story in which three things will change, while C and D prepare together a one minute story in which three things will change, i.e. A prepares to tell the story then B prepares to tell the same story as A but with the three things changed. 3–5 minutes
2. A tells C and B tells D. 1 minute
3. C and D then talk together to try to find the three differences between the stories they have been told, while A and B listen silently to C and D. After three minutes, C and D say what they think the three things are, and A and B tell them. 3 minutes
4. C tells A C's story while D tells B D's version of the story. 1 minute
5. A and B then confer to discover the three differences. 3 minutes

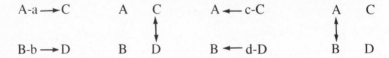

Simulation 35: Alibi! (26 minutes)

1. In new groups of four (A B C and D), A and B prepare an alibi — an exact account of what they were doing together between 6 and 7 p.m. the day before when a murder was committed. Meanwhile C and D are police officers, preparing questions to ask A and B about the time in question. C prepares to question A and D prepares to question B. 5 minutes
2. C questions A while D questions B. A and B must not be able to see or hear each other. 3 minutes

3. C and D compare the answers they get, thus testing the alibis of A and B. A and B compare the answers they gave. 3 minutes

4. C and D confront A and B with the inconsistencies or contradictions, each of which earns A and B five years in jail. 2 minutes

5. Repeat steps 1 to 4 with C and D making their alibi together A and B as police officers. 13 minutes

Discussion 35: Suspects (38–40 minutes)

1. Send six students out of the classroom. They are suspects and they have eight minutes to agree an alibi of what they were all doing together the day before between 6 and 7 p.m. when a murder occurred. Meanwhile, discuss with the rest of the class, who are police officers, what questions to ask to catch the six students out. The police officers are also aiming to accuse one of the six of actually committing the murder. The police gather into six groups and agree on the questions they will ask. There is an empty chair in each group for the suspect. (If possible, the six empty chairs should be in a big circle, facing the walls so that the suspects can't see or hear one another.) 14 minutes

2. Call in the six suspects. They split up so that there is one in each group being questioned. After exactly three minutes, move all the suspects round to be questioned by another group and so on until each group has questioned all six suspects. 18 minutes

3. Send all the suspects out of the room to compare stories, while each police group decides who they think did the murder (e.g. whose story was most different from the other suspects). 3 minutes

4. Call in the suspects. They stand in a row for all to see. Each group of police then accuses one (or two) suspects and briefly explains why. 6 minutes

5. The suspect accused by most police officers is then sentenced to jail. 1 minute

6. Finish with a general discussion. 3–5 minutes

Activity 36 Countries

Topic: Four countries

Words: Places, customs, names

Grammar: Have got

Function: Personal details

Preparation: A world map

A   English-speaking countries (7 minutes)

1. It is better to do this activity after you have taught a song from each of four different English-speaking countries. Show the world map, and brainstorm the names of English-speaking countries (allow mother tongue names and simply translate them), writing them on the map. 3 minutes
2. The class chooses four English-speaking countries they know about, e.g. England, Ireland, Scotland, Wales or USA, Canada, India, Australia. The students make four equal groups and each group decides which country they are (so that all four countries are represented). 1 minute
3. Each group brainstorms in their group all that they know about their country and people. 3 minutes

B   New identity (5–9 minutes)

1. All the groups chant at the same time the names of their country ten times. (They can then sing the song they know for four extra minutes). In silence for one minute each student 'becomes' a person from that country, giving themselves a name, place to live, job, etc. 2 minutes
2. Each group joins another group and makes pairs, e.g. the 'English' join the 'Irish' and make pairs while the 'Scots' join the 'Welsh'. They ask each other about their countries. 3 minutes

C   'My country' (5 minutes)

1. In new groups of four, with one student from each country, the students ask questions and tell each other about their countries. 5 minutes

Role-play, simulation and discussion 36

Topic: Four countries

Words: Holidays and tours

Grammar: Futures, modals

Function: Planning, reporting on plans

Role-play 36: Country visit (8 minutes)

1. In new pairs, (still 'being' the people from the countries as in Activities 36A, 36B and 36C) the students arrange to visit each other's countries and discuss the two visits as holidays and tours. 5 minutes
2. In groups of four with a pair from the other two countries, they report on the holidays they have planned. 3 minutes

Simulation 36: Holiday plans (8 minutes)

1. In new pairs the students are themselves. They plan a holiday together where they will go to one, two, three or four English-speaking countries. 5 minutes
2. In groups of four the pairs report on the holidays they have planned. 3 minutes

Discussion 36 (13–20 minutes)

1. In groups of six the students discuss what people from specific English-speaking countries would like to see and do on holiday in the country your class is in. Each six plans a tour. 8 minutes
2. Each six reports to the whole class. 5–10 minutes

Alternatively:

1. The groups of six quickly draw the world map, and plan a world tour for themselves using at least ten different kinds of transport. 8–10 minutes
2. Each six reports to the whole class. 5–10 minutes

Activity 37 Poems

Topic: Any poems

Words: Any vocabulary

Grammar: Any grammar

Function: Any function

Preparation: Two short poems so each pair has one poem

A Poem mime (10 minutes)

1. Divide the class into two groups X and Y. In each group the students form pairs. Give poem x to each pair in group X. Give poem y to each pair in group Y. Each pair prepares to mime their poem, then to read it aloud. 5 minutes
2. X pairs and Y pairs make fours and each pair mimes their poem, then reads it aloud, then shows the text. 5 minutes

B Combined poems (11 minutes)

1. In the same groups of four, the students combine the two poems to make a story. They can change anything and add anything. They prepare to tell their story. 8 minutes
2. The fours make eights and each four tells their story. 3 minutes

C Ten word performance (15–27 minutes)

1. Each group of eight chooses ten words from the poems. They practise saying them aloud, clapping the rhythm of the words, and saying them in lots of different ways. 4 minutes
2. Tell them they can add two more words of their own, and they must prepare to make a 'musical' performance out of the twelve words. They can say each word more than once. 3 minutes
3. Each four in turn performs their twelve words to the whole class. (They can be judged, e.g. as in the Eurovision Song Contest. 5–8 extra minutes.) 8–12 minutes

Role-play, simulation and discussion 37

Topic: Poems and plays

Words: Any vocabulary

Grammar: Any grammar

Function: Making plays and poems

Role-play 37: Dialogues (14 minutes)

1. In the same groups of eight, the students divide into fours. Each four uses the twelve words to make a dialogue or play, e.g. 8−20 lines. The words must all appear in the dialogue or play. They prepare to perform the dialogue/play. 5 minutes
2. Each four performs to two other fours but *not* to the other four from their eight. 4 minutes
3. The two fours from each eight get back together and perform to each other. 5 minutes

Simulation 37: Poems (13 minutes)

1. Each student writes a poem from their imagination or experience. 8 minutes
2. In groups of three they perform their poem and talk about it. 5 minutes

Discussion 37 (10 minutes)

1. In new groups of six the students discuss the poems they have written. 10 minutes

Activity 38 Hobbies

Topic: Magazines for hobbies

Words: Hobbies

Grammar: Present simple, past simple

Function: Narrating

Preparation: English hobby magazines — one every two students (or divide the magazine so that each pair has four pages each). (The students could answer advertisements and get sample brochures and magazines in the post.)

A   Magazines (4 minutes)

1. Display the magazines (e.g. computer, photography, food, animals, home, gardens, bicycles, cars, love, fashion). In groups of three sharing an interest the students choose a magazine and look through it together. 3 minutes

B   Read an article (11 minutes)

1. Each group of three decides on a particular article or set of pictures and help each other understand it. 8 minutes
2. Each group of three shows the article/pictures to another group and talks about it. 3 minutes

C   Personalise the article (10 minutes)

1. The same group of three chooses that article again, or another article or pictures, and they adapt the article or pictures so that it is about themselves. They prepare to tell the story about themselves. 5 minutes
2. Each group of three tells the story about themselves to three other groups in turn while showing them the article or pictures. 5 minutes

Role-play, simulation and discussion 38

Topic: Magazines for hobbies

Words: Hobbies, shops

Grammar: Question and answer, present simple, comparatives

Function: Shopping, buying, selling, arguing

Role-play 38: Ads (25 minutes)

1. In the same group of three the students look carefully at the advertisements in a magazine. They each prepare to talk about a different product. 4 minutes
2. Half the groups are shop assistants. The other half are customers. For exactly three minutes each group of customers goes into a shop, where the three assistants try to sell them products.
3. At your signal, each group of customers goes into a different shop for three minutes.
4. At your signal each group of customers goes into a third shop for three minutes.
5. The shop assistants and customers swap roles and repeat steps 2 to 4. 9 minutes
6. In new groups of three or four the students say what they 'bought' or didn't 'buy'. 3 minutes

Simulation 38: Spending a fortune (8 minutes)

1. In silence each student prepares to talk about their hobby and how they would spend $1000 or £500 on their hobby (they can share a magazine). 3 minutes
2. In groups of three each student is questioned by the other two, saying only what they want to say in response to questions. They can show the magazine articles, advertisements and pictures to help answer the questions. 5 minutes

Discussion 38: Persuasion (10 minutes)

1. In new groups of four each student tries to persuade the others that their hobby is best. 10 minutes

Activity 39 Songs, poems, texts 2

Topic: Song/poem/text

Words: Any vocabulary

Grammar: Any grammar

Function: Any function

Preparation: A song/poem/text

A Words they like (4—13 minutes)

1. Read aloud or play the song, poem or text while the students listen. 1—4 minutes
2. Read or play it again. This time the students listen for words they like. 1—4 minutes
3. Read or play it again. When the students hear a word they like, they say it aloud during the reading/playing. 1—4 minutes
4. In pairs the students tell each other the words they liked. 1 minute

B Using the words (10 minutes)

1. The pairs have five minutes to create something from the words they liked, e.g. a poem, a song, a story, some sentences, a dialogue.
2. The pairs go round showing/saying/performing to the others what they have created. 5 minutes

C Hearing the text (5—20 minutes)

1. Read aloud or play the song, poem or text with your students singing/saying it with you. Leave occasional gaps or quiet parts which they can fill in. 1—4 minutes
2. Do it again, leaving more gaps and in different places. 1—4 minutes
3. Do it again, mostly leaving gaps. 1—4 minutes
4. Your students sing/recite the whole thing twice without any help. 2—8 minutes

Role-play, simulation and discussion 39

Topic: Song/poem/text

Words: Any vocabulary

Grammar: Any grammar

Function: Any function

Role-play 39: The performance (10–25 minutes)

1. By now the students know the song/poem/text by heart. In groups of two or three they choose one verse/paragraph/section so that all the parts of the song/poem/text are being worked on. They prepare to perform it with creative and imaginative elements (e.g. with full sound effects, acted out, with dramatic music and film effects, as an extended story or as an interview). 5–15 minutes
2. Each group in turn performs their verse/paragraph/section in the order they occur in the song/poem/text. 5–10 minutes

Simulation 39: Personalising the text (15–35 minutes)

1. Each student selects a partner. Together they work on the song/poem/text as a whole in order to express themselves as two individuals. They prepare to display or perform what they create. 10–20 minutes
2. Each pair goes round the other pairs performing or displaying what they have created. 5–15 minutes

Discussion 39: Personal response (5–25 minutes)

1. In groups of six the students discuss and share their different responses to the song/poem/text. 5–25 minutes

Indexes

The numbers given refer to the activities

Vocabulary Index

Grammar Index

Function Index